365

WAYS TO MAKE MONEY

Ideas for quick $ every day of the year

Kylie Ofiu

Wrightbooks

First published 2011 by Wrightbooks
an imprint of John Wiley & Sons Australia, Ltd
42 McDougall Street, Milton Qld 4064

Office also in Melbourne

Typeset in Berkeley LT 11.3/14.5 pt

© Kylie Ofiu 2011

The moral rights of the author have been asserted

National Library of Australia Cataloguing-in-Publication data:

Author:	Ofiu, Kylie, 1985-
Title:	365 ways to make money/Kylie Ofiu.
ISBN:	9780730376217 (pbk.)
Notes:	Includes index.
Subjects:	Small business—Economic aspects—Popular works.
	Self-employed.
Dewey number:	338.642

Cover design by Peter Reardon, Pipeline Design <www.pipelinedesign.com.au>

Cover images: iStockphoto/© Robyn Mackenzie; © Korn, 2011. Used under license from Shutterstock.com.

Author photo: <www.cheekychickenphotography.com.au>.

Printed in China by Printplus Limited

10 9 8 7 6 5 4 3 2 1

Disclaimer

The material in this publication is of the nature of general comment only, and does not represent professional advice. It is not intended to provide specific guidance for particular circumstances and it should not be relied on as the basis for any decision to take action or not take action on any matter which it covers. Readers should obtain professional advice where appropriate, before making any such decision. To the maximum extent permitted by law, the author and publisher disclaim all responsibility and liability to any person, arising directly or indirectly from any person taking or not taking action based upon the information in this publication.

Contents

About the author

As one of nine children, Kylie spent her childhood years in Tasmania and Canberra. Her father taught her about money from a young age and she has always had an interest in it. Doesn't everyone in some way or another?

Throughout her life, Kylie has done the usual things, such as get an education, get a job, get married, get a house and have a family. It was after her second child was born, however, that she become anxious about how she would go back to work with a young family. She came to realise that there had to be a better way to make more money and pay off the mortgage sooner. She wanted to enjoy her children and be at home for them and at the same time make money to help provide for them.

One day she decided to write a list of all the ways she could make money. She asked friends and family and wrote about it on her blog <www.kylieofiu.com>. She originally started with 101 ideas, but the list kept growing. That's how this book was born.

She now lives in Sydney with her husband and two daughters doing what she loves.

How to use this book

You can read the ideas contained in this book from cover to cover if you like. Alternatively you can select chapters relevant to your needs and interests. This book is not just a long list of ideas. Each idea explains what it entails and there are symbols in place to help you know at a glance if the idea suits your needs, such as whether you can put an idea into practice from home, if you need qualifications or money to start and so on.

Following is the symbol system used in this book:

This house is placed next to ideas that you can action from home.

This graduation cap is placed next to ideas you may or definitely do need qualifications for.

This single dollar sign is placed next to ideas that have a start-up cost but it is under $200.

 These dollar signs are placed next to ideas where you will need to spend money before you can make money.

 This mouse symbol is placed next to ideas that you will need a computer for.

 This rating is placed next to ideas that children (anyone under 18 years) could undertake.

 This warning sign is placed under any idea that might be dangerous and caution should be taken.

These symbols make it easy to quickly narrow down ideas that suit you so you can create a shortlist of ideas that you would like to pursue. If an idea appears without a symbol, it means that the option has no restrictions or requirements and you can begin work as soon as you are ready.

Once you have decided on some ideas, research to see if there are any legalities involved with starting that idea in your area. Some areas may require you to register a business name and an ABN. You might also need council approval for any work you do in your home. Since every area is different, there is no specific advice in regards to council requirements and any legal stipulations. It is up to you to do that research.

The prices of what you may earn for each idea will vary from area to area, too, and it is up to you to do a price comparison for where you live and the demand for your service.

If you would like more information about these ideas or how to get them happening, visit my website <www.kylieofiu.com>.

Getting started

Getting started with your money-making endeavour needn't cost a lot. There are a few basic things you will need to do before anything else, but most of it can be done very cheaply. Here are some steps for getting started.

⇨ *Create a proper business plan.* Even if you don't end up sticking to the plan, you need to have one. A business plan usually contains the following elements:

  ◻ *Introduction.* This describes what your business is about. It also outlines your mission statement and goals for the business.

  ◻ *Market research.* This looks at the industry you are going into and how you fit within it.

- *Marketing plan.* This outlines how you are going to advertise your business and get it out there.

- *Operational plan.* This explains how you will set up your business; where it will operate from; regulations, protocol and so on; as well how you will manage your business.

- *Financial plan.* This explains how you are going to fund your business and keep it profitable.

- *Executive summary.* Although this appears on the front page of your business plan, it can't be written until you have completed your entire plan.

▷ *Get legal advice.* It is really easy to check with your local council that what you want to do is legally fine. Ensure you know the ins and outs of every legality applicable to your business or money-making idea and that you will be complying with all laws.

▷ *Speak to an accountant.* They will explain what can be claimed on tax and what advantages there are to setting up your business in a certain way, such as claiming some of your mortgage if you have a home office, claiming work equipment if you use a computer and claiming petrol because you use your car for business purposes. They can also let you know if any government grants are appropriate for you.

▷ *Register for an ABN and a business name.* If you are doing anything that will be more than a hobby, you will need an ABN and a registered business name. You can get an ABN by going to <www.abr.gov.au> and filling out some forms. To register your business name you need to contact the Department of Fair Trading in your state.

⮊ *Apply for government grants.* Now that you are pretty well set up and know what you are doing it is easier to apply for government-sponsored business grants.

⮊ *Get insurance.* There are a variety of companies out there, so you should be able to find one that suits your needs. Public liability insurance can be costly but may be required if you deal with the general public during your money-making ventures.

⮊ *Set proper business hours.* Remember that when you are working for yourself, there are things to do behind the scenes, such as paperwork, quotes and banking, outside of work hours. You need to be clear about the hours your business will operate, when you will do your paperwork and what time will be for family. You don't want the business to consume your life.

⮊ *Get a website.* If you are serious about starting a business, you need a website. You can get a domain name for as little as $6.95 and hosting packages for $1.95 a month. By doing a little research it can be very cheap to set one up. Alternatively, you could set up a free blog, which can be done at websites such as <www.blogger.com> and <www.wordpress.com> until you can switch to a real website. Both websites allow you to make the blog a domain for a small fee at any time.

Five things you need to become a millionaire

Making money is not the only way to become a millionaire. You need to know how to manage your money. There are many people out there on very large salaries who live from pay cheque to pay cheque and others who live on the poverty line who still manage to save! How is that possible?

The following list outlines the main things you need to do, along with some qualities you need to possess or cultivate within yourself, to successfully save money and become a millionaire (or whatever you would like):

➽ put together a budget

➽ be able to stick to your budget and resist temptation

🠒 be motivated

🠒 set a definite goal

🠒 know where and when to get advice.

Put together a budget

Having a budget is quite important. You need to spend less than you earn so you can save to invest and become a millionaire. If you are spending more than you earn, no matter how much you earn you will always spend more than you earn. You need to sit down, work out your expenses versus income, see where you can cut back and make sure you are physically putting savings away every time you get paid.

Be able to stick to your budget and resist temptation

Self-discipline is a problem for many people. As you are saving and trying to become a millionaire you need to have the self-discipline to say 'no' to yourself. Most people can write out a budget but they have problems saying no to themselves when they see something they want to buy because 'They've worked hard and they deserve it'. I am not saying you don't deserve things, but you don't need everything you want or see. Every time I get paid I allow a little to blow on anything I like. If there is something that costs more than I allocate for myself each pay, I have to save for it.

It is a hard skill to cultivate. For some it comes naturally but for most it is difficult. There are a few things you can do to help change your thinking.

⤷ If you are paying off any sort of debt, such as a car loan or mortgage, use a loan amortisation calculator to determine how much difference you will make by paying an extra lump sum—for example, $5, $10 or $20—off your loan. For my current mortgage I pretty much have to multiply the total amount by five. Knowing that a $5 takeaway in reality costs $25 makes it a whole lot less appealing.

⤷ Set yourself a goal and work towards it. Would you prefer to be a millionaire/own your own home/have a holiday or would you prefer that $40 top? If you have a goal in mind, it is much easier to say no to things.

⤷ Calculate how long you will have to work to afford that item. If you get say $20 per hour after tax, you will have to work for two hours to get that $40 top. Do you really want to do that?

⤷ Train yourself to think 'I'll get it later' or 'I don't feel like it', not 'I can't afford it'. It's a hard balance to strike between thinking like a millionaire, where you can pretty much afford whatever you want, and thinking frugally. Thinking 'I can't afford it' is not conducive to a millionaire mindset, but buying everything you want is not conducive to becoming a millionaire. It is all about balance.

Be motivated

Some people are go-getters, others are followers. To become a millionaire you need to cultivate motivation. As you follow your dream of becoming a millionaire you will encounter many obstacles and be faced with a lot of negativity and opposition. You need the motivation to push through and achieve your goal. Lack of motivation is extremely detrimental to achieving anything.

It's not always easy to be motivated, so finding what will motivate you helps. Are there any blogs you like to read, friends who are like-minded, books you have found stimulating or websites you like to visit? You need to find the motivation within yourself, but knowing some external motivational sources that make you feel energised and inspired really works.

Set a definite goal

Goal setting is crucial. You won't be able to stick to a budget and practise self-discipline if you have no goal. Goals need to be SMART:

⇨ Specific

⇨ Measurable

⇨ Achievable

⇨ Relevant

⇨ Time-bound.

Be specific. Clearly define your goal. For example, my goal is to become a millionaire in cash and assets by the time I am 30 in April 2015. My goal is specific with a definite purpose. It's measureable, because I will be able to see clearly if I have enough cash and assets via bank statements and property valuations. It is achievable. Not everyone would agree, but I honestly believe it can be done in a much shorter time frame. It's relevant. Being relevant means it applies to me and serves a purpose. I want to be a millionaire to provide my family with more stability and to help others. It is time-bound because I will do it by the time I am 30. I have five years to go.

So instead of just saying 'I want to be a millionaire', I have set a SMART goal to become a millionaire in cash and assets by the time I am 30 in April 2015. See the difference?

But setting the goal is one thing. You then need to work out an action plan to achieve it. Set subgoals to break your goal into bite-size measurable chunks to keep you on track.

Once you have your goals and action plan, put them where you can read them every day. I keep a copy in my wallet, on my computer and on my blog, and some people put them on their bathroom mirror or on the back of the toilet door. I also have them as a vision board in my bedroom. You need to read them every day so they are constantly on your mind.

Know where and when to get advice

We can't be expected to know everything. There is so much information out there it is impossible for one brain to hold it all. Thankfully we have the internet and people to seek advice from who have the required training in the areas we are interested in. You need to realise when you need advice or help with your goals and ambitions, then you need to know where to get it. It is incredibly easy to source information on the internet. The information is not always correct, though, so you need to sift through all the material out there and find what it is true and relevant.

There are professionals in every field. By networking you meet people who may know what you need to know or who might connect you with someone who can help. The more people you meet the higher the chance of them knowing something or someone of relevance to you. If you apply these principles to your life, you will be well on your way.

Part 1

MAKE MONEY

FROM HOME

In this section you will find a variety of ways to make money from home. The first ideas can be done without much effort and can be completed on top of anything else you do. Further in this section you will find ideas that can pretty much be done from home, although you will need to leave the house sometimes.

Many of these ideas can also be combined, which will enable you to make more money with very little effort.

1   Rent a room to a boarder

Renting a room to a boarder can be one of the fastest and easiest ways to make money. It is also something that requires very little effort providing you begin with a good agreement.

You will need to advertise your room stating whether it is furnished or not, if you accept males or females, smokers or nonsmokers only and so on. The ads can be placed in the classifieds of a newspaper, in university newsletters or online. There are lots of free and cheap websites now that accept advertisements for rooms for rent, such as <www.gumtree.com.au>.

When you get applicants, host interviews asking all the questions you can think of and lay down the ground rules. If someone doesn't feel right, trust your instincts.

If you have a furnished room, you can charge more than the base rate. You could also offer meals for a set fee. Depending on where you live you can expect to rent your room out for $100 to in excess of $200 per week.

2   Host an exchange student

Hosting an exchange student can be a lot easier than finding a boarder in many ways. There are usually three different types of agreements with student exchanges, where you provide:

- ▷ just room
- ▷ room and meals
- ▷ room, meals and transport.

As a host parent you may need to help set the student up with a bank account, show them around your area and teach them various aspects about the local culture. If you are a host family, it is best to live near schools and good public transport to make it easier for the student to get around.

You will need to do your research as not all programs pay the host family. For information look online or contact universities and international schools in your area.

Most exchange students pay $170 to $220 a week for room and meals.

 ## 3 Rent your house out while you're on holidays

A great way to earn a little while you are on holidays is to rent your house out. Often over the Christmas break and school holidays friends have families visiting and may not be able to accommodate them. This option offers those people cheaper accommodation than a hotel room and it will help you pay the mortgage while you are away.

You will need to discuss the ground rules, the cost of rent and bond, if pets are allowed, if smoking is acceptable and so on. It is a good idea to lock away and store anything you do not want used or accessed. Most people won't rifle through your things, but it will put your mind at ease.

Depending on where you live you could make between $300 to $500 a week, or even more if you own a coastal property.

Rent your house to film and TV companies

If you live close to where films and TV shows are produced, you could offer your home as a location for scenes. Since your home will not be used all day every day it can be a great way to make a bit of cash.

Film companies often want a house for contracts of nine months or more, with access to it pretty much whenever they like—day or night—but your house is unlikely to be used every day during that period.

TV shows are usually filmed seasonally, and again it is unlikely that your house would be needed for every episode, so it might only be for a few days here and there. Commercials usually only take between one and two days to film.

Be aware that they may want to make alterations to your home and that there is a chance your house may get damaged during filming. Also having lots of people, trucks and cars in the street may upset your neighbours.

The best way to begin is to contact a location scout who will check out your house and area if they are interested. For a complete list of location scouts around Australia, have a look at <http://www.kftv.com/product-country-3580-AUS. html>.

You can make in excess of $500 a day for TV ads. If your property has amazing views, you can earn thousands of dollars a day. It's all about what people are looking for.

5 Rent your attic or basement for storage

If you have a large attic or basement you don't use, you could rent it to people needing storage. You would need to work out a good agreement, including when whoever is renting can access their belongings, what can and can't be stored, how much notice you require before a visit, how much you will charge and the length of the contract, how far in advance payments need to be made and what happens if they stop paying.

Commercial storage can be expensive but the advantage is that people can access their belongings anytime they want. However, if someone is travelling for a few months and needs to store their things while they're away, your basement can be a great option.

You will need a proper written contract. You will also need to check with your insurance company to see if their belongings are covered under your policy or if they will need to organise their own insurance. This idea is great if you know people looking to store stuff, so start by asking around, or put an ad in your local paper or on a community noticeboard.

You could make $20 to $50 a week, depending on how much is being stored and for how long.

6 Rent your garage

This is similar to renting your attic or basement, with the difference being that it's easier for the renter to access their stuff without interrupting your life. They can have a key to the garage door and come and get things as required.

As per renting your attic or basement, you will need a contract stating rules such as how much can be stored, costs, insurance and when they can access their belongings. You can advertise online through a free website such as <www.gumtree.com.au>.

You could charge in excess of $30 depending on how much is being stored and for how long, and what the cost is to rent storage units in your area.

7 Rent your driveway for caravans or boats

If you have a large driveway or even space on your lawn, you could rent it to someone who owns a caravan or boat but has nowhere to store it.

The renters would need their own insurance for their vehicle, plus a cover for a boat as it will be sitting out in all kinds of weather. They will also need to let you know when they will be using the caravan or boat so you don't come home one day and think it has been stolen.

You could charge $20 to $50 a week depending on where you live.

8 Rent your driveway as parking space

If you live near office buildings or in the city, you could offer your driveway for rent to people who work nearby. Not everyone gets parking access with their job and not everyone catches public transport. In some cities parking can be very expensive.

Besides receiving money for this service, another advantage for you is that thieves will be deterred by a car parked in your driveway.

Contact the companies that may have interested employees and ask if you can send an email to their staff. A short description of your offer plus contact details is all that is needed. You will also need to check with your council that you are allowed to do this.

Depending on your location you can charge from $5 a day per car. If you have the space, you can always rent to more than one person.

  9 ## Rent your front lawn or driveway if you live near a stadium or showground

If you live near a stadium or showground, you could rent driveway space to those attending. This will have great appeal if your rate is cheaper than the surrounding parking facilities, plus getting out of these places can take forever and be a real nightmare.

All you need to do is put a sign out the front of your house and have a few flyers available. It is then up to people to approach you if they are interested in using your driveway. They need to pay upfront, so you have to be around when people are looking for parking.

Some people may want your contact details for events in the future, so be prepared with an email address or phone number written down.

You could charge $5 to $10 depending on your city and the going rates.

10 Run a bed and breakfast

If you have a larger home and don't mind being host to strangers, cooking them dinner and cleaning up after them, this can be a great way to make your home earn money. Bed and breakfasts are not just cottage homes in the country or by the seaside; they can be any home anywhere.

It is up to you to decide the services you will provide, such as just breakfast or a dinner option as well, daily turn down service, single or group rooms and an ensuite or shared bathroom.

You will need to check with your council regarding the permits you will need, but once it is all up and running the opportunity and options are endless. To get started there are a variety of places you can advertise online, such as <www.bedandbreakfast.com.au>. You can select your state and join to advertise your bed and breakfast. Contact travel agents and offer to have them stay for a free trial so they recommend your home, and email everyone you know with a special deal or discount if they recommend you to their friends.

Depending on where your home is located you could charge anything from $100 a night.

11 Use your swimming pool for classes

Qualifications to teach swimming or water aerobics are essential, but once you have them you can use your pool for a variety of options. A few possibilities include learning to swim classes for kids and adults, water aerobic classes, water exercises for people with a disability, or even hydrotherapy for those who have had accidents or injuries.

You will need to contact your council to ensure you meet the necessary requirements. Also check your insurance policy to see if you need separate or increased coverage.

Classes can start at $7 for kids' swimming lessons and increase to $10 to $15 for a water aerobics class.

12 Rent your swimming pool

If you don't have swim teaching qualifications or have no interest in giving classes, you could lease your pool to someone who does. You will need to set up an agreement including information such as the times they can use the pool, how much it will cost, their insurance details and what other parts of the house are free to use (for example, toilets and bathrooms).

To find suitable applicants you could contact your local TAFE or swimming institutions, as students may be interested once they have their qualifications. You could advertise in your local newspaper, or just talk to other mums, friends, family members and people in your community. You never know who might know someone who's interested.

You could charge the instructor $5 or more per hour or a set weekly fee. It is up to both of you to decide what you think is fair.

13 Lease garden allotments

Many people would like to grow their own food or pretty flowers but do not have the space to do so. There are some community groups who garden in a shared space quite successfully now. If you have the space available, it is an excellent way to develop a community spirit in your area.

Generally those interested pay an annual fee to lease a small garden plot plus a per square metre annual fee. Some people provide sheds as well as individual fencing, and some provide all the gardening tools required as well. It is up to you to decide what you offer and what gardeners need to bring.

You will need to set clear rules, such as if a gardener does not use their plot for a certain period of time it can be re-let. You will also need to check your insurance policy to see if you have adequate coverage.

Depending on how many plots you have available, you could make a few hundred dollars a year for this service.

14 Display signs on your fence

If you live on a busy street, you could display signs for businesses on your fences. It is great exposure for the businesses and you don't need to do anything except allow the sign to be put up.

You will need to establish with the business how big the sign can be, how long it will be up for, how it is to be removed, what is allowed to appear on the sign and what happens if the sign gets graffitied.

If this interests you, contact some local businesses to see if they are keen. A small newspaper ad can cost more than $100, so a larger sign on your fence will be a more cost-effective way for businesses to advertise. You could charge businesses $50 or more a week.

1 5 Complete online surveys

There are lots of horror stories about people doing surveys for hours and not getting paid anything or being paid a measly five cents. Online surveys will not make you rich and I do not know of anyone who really makes a full-time wage from doing surveys online.

That said, there are still plenty of legitimate online survey websites who will pay you, such as <www.pureprofile.com. au> or <www.yourvoice.com.au>. Generally you get sent the surveys or have to log in every day. You will be told if there is a survey available, how long it is and how much you will get paid, so you can choose whether or not to do it.

Signing up can sometimes be quite long because the companies want to know everything about you to ensure they send you relevant surveys, but once you have signed up the process is pretty easy.

You will most likely only earn $20 to $100 a month doing this work. Some survey websites pay in the form of gift cards instead of cash.

16 Be a product tester

Some companies need people to test new products and provide an opinion about them. You sign up to the companies and they will contact you when they have something they want you to test. Some pay with gift cards on top of the free product, but more often than not you simply receive a free product. You will usually get enough products to share between friends and family.

Sometimes after sampling there is a short survey, but often it only takes a minute or so to complete. Have a look at <www.freestuff.com.au> for tips on how to get started. Another good website is <www.soup.com.au>, which will contact you when it has products that suit your profile.

You may only make $5 or so from testing the products, but you could save $20 or more from your usual grocery bill since you won't have to buy those products yourself.

17 Complete product reviews

Product reviews are easy to write and get paid for. The payment is usually in the form of a gift card, the amount of which varies depending on the amount and length of reviews written, and often you get to keep the product you review.

There are websites that you can sign up with to write reviews, such as <www.productreview.com.au>. The reviews usually need to be 50 words to qualify. Each review is allocated points that accrue and you use to redeem gift vouchers.

You can make $20 or more depending on how many reviews you write.

18 Enter competitions

Entering competitions is not a sure way to get money, but you can't win if you don't enter. Not all prizes offered are in cash. Other prizes are in the form of gift cards, TVs, beauty products and so on.

There are competition clubs and websites you can join, such as Win Big Australia or <www.compingclub.com>, which have information about all the competitions currently running that you can enter. The competitions that attract the least amount of entries are usually those that require you to write 25 words or less, as these require a bit of effort.

If you want to enter competitions, keeping good records will be very helpful, so make sure you record each competition entered in a notebook or diary indicating when it was run, what was involved and if you won anything. Make sure you keep your receipts if you are entering a purchasing competition that asks for proof of purchase. And always record your 25 words or less answers, as you will always be able to refer to this to see which answers were successful.

This is not reliable income but you will probably win a few hundred dollars worth of prizes or cash in a year if you enter a lot of competitions.

19 Provide family day care

Looking after children in your home is a great way to make money while not having to leave your house. There are various groups you can sign up with, such as the Australian Child

Care Career Options (ACCCO) or <www.familydaycare. com.au>, which will help you get started, such as with training and assisting you to get your house child proofed. Alternatively, you can organise all of this yourself. The initial set-up can be a bit expensive but you can easily make a full-time wage once you are in operation.

You will need a first-aid certificate, a police check and insurance coverage, as well as your qualification. There are also laws governing how many children can be cared for by one carer, but this can be up to five kids a day. You can be open five days a week or select to operate part time.

The amount you make will vary but you could expect to earn $45 000 or more before tax and expenses.

 ## Receive trailing commissions

Almost everything you do with your money, such as pay your mortgage, personal loan and life insurance, can have a trailing commission attached. This is a small commission, often only a fraction of a percentage of the loan, which is paid to the original broker. There are a variety of companies who will get this money back for you, such as <www.irefund.com.au>.

For a fee you can enlist a company to go over all your financials and redirect these trailing commissions through them and back to you. During the first year you don't make much due to the initial fee but in subsequent years you can make more.

Customers typically get a few hundred to thousands of dollars back a year, depending on how many products they have with trailing fees and just how high those fees are.

21 Join cashback clubs

Websites such as <www.buckscoop.com.au> will let you know which cashback offers are available when you purchase certain products. Sometimes you can try products for free thanks to cashback offers.

Not all cashback offers are for products you have to buy. There are also cashback offers available when you switch banks, talk to a mortgage broker, or switch services such as a telephone or electricity provider. These offers are not always advertised by the companies and can only be redeemed through cashback clubs.

All you have to do is check what is on offer and, if you are interested, sign up for it through the link on the cashback website. It can take a few months to get the cash back, so record the details and keep an eye on it to ensure you get paid.

Depending on the offer you may receive as little as $3 for bread or upwards of $50 for consulting with a mortgage broker.

22 Offer your trailer for hire

Most people who own trailers don't use them every day and they are often just sitting in your garage or driveway. Offering you trailer for hire is a great way to make back registration costs and make it more worthwhile to own the trailer.

If you will be hiring on a small scale, word of mouth is the best way to go. Otherwise advertising with flyers and using community notice boards is a good option. Check that your insurance policy covers you to hire out your trailer, and when you do hire make sure that you get a deposit so that the trailer is returned.

You can make between $20 to $80 per day depending on the size of your trailer.

23 Display trailer wraps

A trailer wrap is advertising on a trailer for a business. The signage on the trailer is a moving advertisement whenever you use the trailer and it can also sit at the front of your house for all to see.

Simply approach some businesses and see if they are interested in advertising with you. If you live in a busy area where the trailer will be seen regularly, or if you use the trailer a lot, the offer will be more attractive.

You could make $50 to $300 a month depending on the size of the signage, where you live and how much traffic is likely to see the trailer wrap.

24 Hold a garage sale

A successful garage sale is not just about putting your old junk on the front lawn and hoping for the best. You need to be organised.

Sort through everything you own. Clean all the items for sale and ensure they are in working order. Make a date for the sale then advertise in the local newspaper and, if your council permits, display signs around your neighbourhood.

Price everything clearly and display them well so things are easy to see and get to. Be careful not to overprice your items. Your goods are only worth what someone else is willing to pay, so be ready to bargain, too.

Make sure you have lots of small change as it is highly likely that the first person who comes will want to pay for a $2 item with a $50 note! Carry cash in a bag on you at all times.

If your area allows, you might also like to bake some muffins to sell, or have a sausage sizzle or sell cold drinks for extra cash.

Generally, if done well and you have a lot of items to sell, you can make a few hundred dollars or more.

25 Grow wheatgrass trays and sell wheatgrass shots

Wheatgrass is really easy to grow and very good for you. One tray will give you about six shots. You need a specific juicer for wheatgrass, but these are not too expensive.

To get started all you need are seedling trays, organic dirt, newspaper and wheat. Sprout the wheat, then prepare the trays. To prepare the trays lay newspaper on the bottom, followed by dirt, then cover with a thin layer of the sprouted wheat. Spray with water and place in a cool dark place to grow (drawers are good). Spray the wheatgrass with water daily to help it grow. Once it is 5 centimetres tall, bring it out into the sun to turn green.

Wheatgrass shots cost around $4 each from a store. Even if you sold your trays for $10 per tray, your customers will get a $14 saving. Alternatively you could sell the shots for $3 each, saving your customers $1. If you work in an office, it would be very easy to sell these to your colleagues. Or you could contact gyms and personal trainers to see if they would be interested for you to sell through them.

Depending on your costs it is easy to make $8 a tray and more for individual shots.

26 Create garden sculptures

There are many different types of sculptures you could make from a variety of objects, such as scrap metal and wood. Selling your sculptures at markets, online or even by approaching small nurseries and similar businesses to see if they are interested is a good way to get started.

Displaying them in your own garden with a sign out the front of your house specifying 'garden sculptures sold here' is another great way to attract business and advertise for free.

Depending on where you source your materials and how much they cost you could make upwards of $40 a sculpture.

27 Sell potted bulbs or herbs

Potted plants sell really well at markets. Bulbs look great when they are flowering, herbs are easy to grow from seed and you could make unique pots, such as bruschetta pots—basil around a tomato plant—or an Italian herbs pot, which is a mix of herbs such as rosemary, sage, marjoram and basil.

You could also sell bare bulbs, just in a bag to be planted in the garden straight away; bulbs multiply under the ground as they grow so they're easy to reproduce.

The type of plant and how it is presented will determine your profit but you could easily make a few dollars from each small seedling pot and up to $50 for a full flowering pot of bulbs.

28 Sell heirloom vegetables

Heirloom vegetables are older style, non-genetically modified vegetables. Often they come in a variety of colours (such as purple carrots), which is a great way to encourage kids to eat their vegetables. The seeds cost a little more than regular seeds but they are very popular vegetables. Since they are unique they sell for a higher price than regular vegetables.

You could sell the seedlings in pots or grow and sell the vegetables. They could be sold at markets or from your house with a sign out the front, or check with small local supermarkets to see if they are interested in stocking them.

Seedlings can be sold from $5 and the vegetables can be sold for $1 more than the regular vegetables.

29 Keep and breed bees

Keeping bees is becoming much more popular with an increasing number of people seeking to be more self-sufficient.

The initial set-up costs can be high, but once you are organised the maintenance costs are minimal. You will need some training to begin with so you know what you are doing and can offer advice to those you will be selling to. For a list of beekeeping associations visit <www.honeybee.com.au/beeinfo/assn.html>.

Once you are up and running you could advertise at markets, or through newspapers or magazines aimed at farming and self-sufficiency, such as Mother Earth News <www.motherearthnews.com>.

It will cost about $500 to set up, but you will be able to sell a colony for $150 to $200. If you sell the hive with it, you can charge another $200, depending on the size of the hive.

 ## sell honey

If you are keeping bees, one of the best ways to make money from them is by selling the honey. Fresh honey tastes so much nicer than the store-bought stuff.

You will need bees and the necessary equipment as well as sterilised jars or plastic tubs. It is up to you how you sell it, whether by the kilo or in small jars. To keep costs down and entice customers back you could offer a discount for refills instead of using new jars.

You can sell the honey at markets, online, to colleagues, friends and family, as well as from your home by advertising out the front. If you package it well, you could approach boutique gift stores, delis or small grocers to see if they would be interested in stocking it. You could sell it for $10 to $15 a kilogram, or $5 for smaller jam jars.

31 Keep and breed chickens

Chickens are relatively easy to keep and not too expensive to get started. You will need a chicken coop, chickens and food; if you are handy, you could make the coop yourself cheaply.

When sourcing chickens you could approach preschools as many of them hatch eggs as part of the curriculum. This can work out much cheaper than buying chicks elsewhere.

There are many varieties of chickens, so you will need to research which breed you would like to raise and sell. You can sell the chickens through newspapers such as *The Land* or online via websites such as <www.gumtree.com.au>.

When selling your chickens they will need to have been laying to get the highest price. Non-egg laying chickens sell for around $10 and egg laying chickens from $15.

32 Sell eggs

Fresh free range eggs taste so much better than store-bought eggs, and they are increasingly in demand. All you need is a chicken coop, a few laying hens and some chook food.

There is not a lot of work involved in keeping chickens. You need to check daily for the eggs, feed the chickens and ensure they have water. There is a variety of breeds and some produce more eggs than others. Hens go 'off the lay' at various times, so you won't get an egg a day from every chicken all year.

You can sell the eggs at markets, to family and friends, or pop a sign at the front of your house. Everyone I know who has sold eggs has never been able to produce enough, as so many people want them.

You could make a few hundred dollars a year with just a few chickens and selling a dozen eggs for $4 to $6.

3 3 Sell compost bins

As society becomes more environmentally aware and more people are turning to gardening, compost bins are becoming increasingly popular.

There are actually a few ways to make money from compost bins—you can make and sell them, buy and resell them, teach people how to use them properly and get the best from them, or sell your own compost if you have plenty.

You can sell them online, at markets, by advertising in the newspaper or self-sufficiency magazines such as *Mother Earth News* <www.motherearthnews.com>, or from your house.

How much you earn depends on the cost of materials or supplies but you could make $50 or more a bin.

3 4 Sell worm farms

Worm farms are similar to compost bins, except they have worms to break down everything faster. Worms eat your food scraps, such as vegetable peels and apple cores, and turn them into great food for your garden. And worms can last for up to six weeks eating damp newspaper when you go on holiday!

You can choose to sell the whole kit, which includes the farm and the worms, or just sell the worms. Most people sell the worms for $40 or more per 1000 worms. You could sell worm farms in the same manner as the compost bins mentioned previously, or even contact your local council to see if you can sell through them. My local council sells compost bins and worm farms for a reasonable price.

Due to the variety of worm farms and worms available, you can make anything from $20 to $150 from selling them.

35 Sell fruit trees

There are so many different varieties of fruit trees. Besides the different types of fruits there are dwarf trees, full size trees, trees that suit pots and grafted fruit salad trees (a tree growing more than one type of fruit).

You can grow fruit trees from seed, which will take a while, or buy small seedlings to grow bigger and sell. If you are growing from seed, you could sell the trees as seedlings, one-year-old trees or as mature trees.

Selling online or at markets is the easiest way, but you could also approach businesses to see if they are interested in selling your trees for you. You could make $10 to $30 a tree depending on your costs involved.

36 Offer an embroidery service

Name embroidery can easily be done from your home or by setting up in your garage. To work on a commercial scale you do need an embroidery machine but it can be quite lucrative. You could embroider names on business uniforms, sports uniforms, towels, bathrobes and more.

To get started contact businesses, schools and sports clubs and offer them a discount. Getting your business out there is the hardest part, but once people know who you are and what you do, you will get a lot of referral work and repeat customers, especially if your work is good.

You could also choose to have a stall at markets with some items such as towels and face washers already embroidered, and offer a personalised service for an extra cost.

Once you have recouped the cost of the embroidery machine you will easily make a few dollars from each item you embroider.

37   Sell Your own art

Selling your own art can be easier said than done, but there are some ways to get more exposure than by just selling to friends and family or selling from a market.

Approach doctors' offices, display homes, cafés or other businesses where artwork is often displayed and ask if you can hang your artwork on a wall with a small sign stating the title of the artwork and its cost.

The benefit works both ways because they won't need to buy artwork and your work will get exposure. You could also offer to change the paintings every few months or whenever a piece is sold. You could also offer them 10 per cent of the sale price as an incentive to keep your artwork on their walls.

Your artwork is personal and the supplies you use will depend on the type of art you create, as will the amount you make. You might earn $50 up to hundreds of dollars for a single painting.

38 Make pregnant belly casts

Anything involving babies is big business and many women want belly casts, which is basically plaster applied to the pregnant stomach that is set. You can then paint them or leave them plain as the white plaster. Popular designs include flowers, sunsets, countries of birth and the parents' hand prints.

You don't need a lot of materials and it can be done from your garage. It's quite easy to learn how to do and the overall process isn't long.

A great place to get started is by linking up with baby shops. Offer a referral fee and leave some flyers with them. Also, creating a Facebook page and linking up with work-at-home parent websites will give your new business great exposure. There are lots of instructions online about belly casting, such as <www.craftbits.com/project/pregnant-belly-casting>.

Belly casts typically start at $150 to make, so you can earn a fair bit once you factor in the cost of supplies. Most people charge $100 extra for designs and artwork.

39 Make baby hand and feet casts

Baby hand and feet casts are very popular and easy to do, if the babies are cooperative. You can work with a business franchise if you prefer not to start on your own. This work is trickier than making pregnant belly casts, so some people offer both services.

If you go with the franchise option, starting up is easy. Franchises such as <www.twinkletoes.com.au/> offer great packages and support. If you go it alone, there are many ways to promote yourself, such as with local mothers' groups, online forums and baby expos.

Most cast imprints start at $120 but can also cost a lot more. After factoring in your supplies, you could earn an average $80 a cast.

 ## Create your own jewellery

There are a few ways you can create your own jewellery. You can make necklaces and earrings from beads right through to unique hand-stamped silver and gold jewellery to pendants revealing all the kids' names or a family tree.

For stamped jewellery there are businesses you can buy a franchise from, such as <www.smallp.com.au>, or just get the supplies and do it yourself. There are a variety of options you can make, such as dog tags, circular family tree pendants or name pendants. Alternatively, beading supplies can be sourced cheaply and you can make your own unique creations—try <www.beadandcrystalheaven.com.au>.

The best ways to promote yourself are via online social networks and by going to markets and expos. Once people know your work, business will pick up. Another option is to approach businesses and ask if they will sell your jewellery either on consignment or by buying your range. Your jewellery can be arranged on a stand to sit on their counter or displayed within the shop.

Hand-stamped pendants usually sell from $65 and take one or two hours to make. Beaded jewellery generally sells for less.

41 Restore furniture

If you are handy, have the tools and the patience, you could restore furniture. Most of the time the work will be a matter of filling a few holes, sanding and lacquering, or it could be as simple as applying a fresh coat of paint. If you wish to restore antiques, it is best to get the experience and knowledge to do so.

If you keep your eye out, you might see furniture to restore cheaply, which you can then resell, or you can restore other people's furniture for a fee.

To advertise, put out flyers and place an ad in your local newspaper. Your best advertisement will be word of mouth, so to get started consider offering to do some work for your friends or family for free or at a big discount. This is a great way to begin a portfolio for customers so they can view the quality of your work. You could make $100 or more per piece of furniture.

42 Build dining tables and chairs

I lived next door to a man once who used to make the most gorgeous dining tables and chairs. He made them out of recycled timber, usually Australian hardwoods, and did it all from home.

It is hard work but if you are good with wood and enjoy it, you can make money. Be on the lookout for ads for free wood in your local newspaper and online, as well as from people who are cutting down their trees. You may be able to get a lot of wood for free, which will be a significant saving.

You could sell your furniture yourself at markets or approach businesses to see if they are interested in stocking your pieces, even on consignment. If you are able to get the wood for free or cheaply, you can easily make $500 for a four-seater dining table.

43   Offer an ironing service

If you enjoy ironing, this can be an easy way to make money. Ironing is loathed by many people, and since most families have both parents working, it's often easier to pay someone else to do it.

You will need a good iron, an ironing board, starch sprays, a clothes rack and spare coathangers. Tell clients they need to supply their own coathangers, but have some on hand just in case. It is best if you are a nonsmoker with no pets, as the smells can get into the clothes and your clients won't appreciate this.

To get started place flyers on community noticeboards and spread the word to your friends and family. It is up to you to charge per basket or per item. If you charge per basket, be specific and state 'flat basket', otherwise people will try to put as much as possible in there. You can also offer a same day service, where people drop their baskets off before work and pick them up on the way home, or an overnight service.

On average you can charge $30 to $50 for a flat basket. Alternatively, for individual items I suggest $2–3 per shirt, $2–5 for pants, and so on.

44 Wash clothes

People are busier than ever these days and want to outsource as much of their housework as possible. Many people will now pay to have their washing done as well.

It is up to you to decide on your level of service—do they drop off or do you pick up, do you offer same day or overnight service and do you iron as well? What about stubborn stains? Do you offer a guarantee? You will need a good washing machine, heavy duty soaking and stain removal products, a clothes dryer and no qualms about touching other people's underwear.

Your main clientele will be the time poor or office workers; these are the first people to approach. You could also offer a pick-up and drop-off service to those who are ill or recovering from an injury. You can make $20 a load, and more for heavy stains and ironing.

45 Pay-per-click sites

There are legitimate pay-per-click sites out there, such as <www.rewardscentral.com.au> and <www.wdyt.com.au>. All you have to do is sign up to them and then log in daily, even a few times a day, and click on whatever they have sent you. Some will send you emails to click on, others will require you to sign into the website to click on paying ads.

You earn usually only 1 cent to 10 cents a click and you need $20 to $50 to get paid, so it can take a while to earn enough to actually see your money. Not all the websites pay cash either; some provide gift cards, so you need to check this before you sign on. You can make $100 or so a year depending on how many sites you click on.

46 Make a Squidoo lens

A Squidoo lens is basically one web page of information on any topic that you like. You go to <www.squidoo.com> and sign up. It's free and it is a step-by-step process, so it's relatively easy. You can place ads on your page for other websites, which is one way your lens/page will earn money. If your lens is popular, Squidoo will pay you as well. A lens can be about anything you like, including photos, YouTube clips and other features. The more pages you make and the more popular your lens, the more money you make.

Some people earn a few dollars, while others earn hundreds and top earners make thousands of dollars on Squidoo. It's up to you.

47 Type résumés

Not everyone is good at writing their own résumé. In fact, a good résumé is crucial in the current job market, so a good résumé service will be highly sought after.

You need to be articulate, with good writing skills, and you need to be able to translate what the client wants to say into what their potential employers will want to read — a job description will help you tailor the résumé. Advertising at universities or in your local newspaper is a good way to get started.

How much you make will vary from area to area but $100 is fairly average.

48 Create a blog

A blog is basically an online diary or 'web log' where you can write anything you like. It doesn't have to be about your life specifically, it can be about anything that you are interested in.

It takes a bit of work to set up a good, user-friendly blog and you need to update it regularly to keep people reading. You can set up your blog for free using a website such as <www.wordpress.com> or <www.blogger.com>.

You make money with a blog through a variety of ways, such as using affiliate marketing, featuring ads from sponsors and Google ads on your blog, selling things you make, creating ebooks or courses, or by direct donation.

To start with you will earn nothing but as your blog increases in popularity and picks up subscribers you can make a few hundred dollars per year and if it's really popular you can make thousands of dollars. Top bloggers make hundreds of thousands of dollars.

49 Type university assignments

If allowed by the university involved, your services could include typing, editing and proofreading assignments and essays. Make it clear that you are not responsible for the grade achieved, as the student is the one who does the research and compiles the work—you simply correct spelling and grammar and fix any layout issues.

Many students feel overwhelmed by their work and paying someone to make their assignment look good can relieve some of their stress. For many, the removal of spelling and grammatical errors in their work may be the difference between a pass and fail.

Contact your local university to see if you can offer your service to its students. You might be able to put signage up around the university or include a listing in a newsletter or orientation packages.

You could charge $10 per page for editing and $5 per page for proofreading. Set a page minimum so you don't end up working on just small assignments. You could make approximately $200 per assignment.

50 Become an editor

There are so many things that need editing, from small publications such as business newsletters and school assignments right through to bigger publications such as books, magazines and websites. You could edit for freelance journalists, bloggers and website owners.

You must have an eye for detail and a good command of the written language All the equipment you really need is a computer and an internet connection.

Advertise your services with a flyer at universities and email businesses to see if you can edit their newsletters. Another way to generate work is to contact websites that contain errors in their copy to see if they are interested in paying you to show them their errors.

Depending on the size of the editing job, you could make a few hundred dollars to thousands of dollars for each project.

5 1 Type medical transcripts

Medical transcribing requires some training, but even after paying for and completing your training you will more than likely earn back anything you paid within six months of working. You can pick the hours you want to work and work for yourself or for an agency.

Your work will require typing what doctors have voice recorded. It can take up to four hours to type one hour of recorded voice, so it can be rather slow.

To find work check the employment classifieds in newspapers. Even if full-time work is being advertised you can at least offer the hours you are willing to work until someone full-time can be employed. This will get your foot in the door and will help you get a reference. Generally you can earn upwards of $25 an hour.

52 Prepare transcripts for businesses

The medical field isn't the only type of business that needs material transcribed. Many other businesses, such as law firms, also require it. For basic transcribing you just need to have a good typing speed and be proficient in computer programs such as MYOB, Word, Excel and Publisher. As long as you know how to use these programs properly you should be able to get work. You don't need specialised training, unlike for medical transcripts.

You can find work through employment classifieds in news-papers or online. Some businesses will employ you full time, while others are happy for you to choose your own hours. Having a website to promote yourself can help, but isn't essential. You can earn $25 or more an hour; some solicitors pay around $8 per page.

53 Offer affiliate marketing

Affiliate marketing is done online via a website or blog. You can do it to a small degree on Facebook and other social networking sites. Affiliate marketing is when you recommend a product on your website and each time a person clicks on that product's link and then buys that product you receive a commission from the affiliate program you have signed with.

There are lots of programs that you can do affiliate marketing with, from financial products to books to make-up. All you need to sign up as an affiliate is go to any website that sells a product, such as <www.fishpond.com.au>, click on the link that says affiliates and join its program. You will then be issued with a link, which you place on your blog, website or on your Twitter or Facebook profile. When people click on the links you get a set amount. Many affiliate accounts require that you reach a certain amount before payout, such as $50 worth of affiliate sales.

The amount you make is completely dependent upon how many people buy through you and how much they spend. It might be $10 here and there, or you might make thousands of dollars.

54   Create and sell an ebook

U18

An ebook is a book that appears online and can be downloaded to your computer or ebook reader. To create an ebook you can write about anything you like, convert it into a PDF document and then sell it either via your own website or on a website that sells books, such as <www.amazon. com> (go to the self-publish link at the bottom of the website for options). An ebook won't sell for as much as a normal printed book, but they are increasingly popular.

If you have your own website or blog, you can sell your ebook through programs such as <www.e-junkie.com>. You sign up, load your book, then put the link on your site. People can then buy it and download it by clicking on the link and you pay as little as $5 a month for this service.

The hardest part about selling an ebook is not usually the writing but the promoting. You need to promote it everywhere. A good option is to offer an affiliate scheme for bloggers to promote it so everyone knows about it when it is launched.

Depending on what your ebook is about, how popular it is, how big it is and how you decided to sell it, you can make thousands by selling it for between $5 to $50.

55 Become a virtual assistant

A virtual assistant does administrative duties for people. They work from their own premises and do everything online, such as bookwork when people require it, taking telephone calls or answering emails, but are not always hired as a full-time employee. This arrangement suits a lot of businesses.

You need to have excellent computer skills and administrative experience because there is no on-the-job training—you have to do it all. You need to provide your own equipment, such as a computer, internet facility and telephone, and you will need to work out your own taxes because you are a private contractor, not an employee.

To get started you could either check newspaper employment classifieds or contact real estate agents, solicitors, insurance agents, doctors and anyone else you think might be interested. Give them a detailed outline of what you do and the prices you charge. You can make $20 to $70 an hour depending on your services and experience.

56 Create a local business website

If there isn't already one for your area, you could create a website to support your local businesses. Local businesses will pay to have a spotlight article written about them, or it could just be an information website with affiliate ads and links.

It could contain a section where people publish reviews of the businesses, as well as a section for local businesses to offer sales products, or a discount code if a person finds a business through your website. The website could cover your own town only or you could make it statewide and people can select their area of interest.

If it goes well, you could make a few hundred to a few thousand dollars each month from advertising.

5 7 Personalised storybooks

This is a business you can buy into and quickly make back what you have spent. Personalised storybooks are books where people give you the details they want, such as their child's name, and then that name is used in a story with a character of their choice, such as Tinkerbell or Superman. Another option is to create personalised letters from Santa during the Christmas period.

Once you have bought into the business you could contact schools, kindergartens, childcare centres and junior sporting clubs to see if they are interested in using your business for fundraising. It will get your name out there and provide quite a few orders.

For more information, visit <www.bestpersonalizedbooks. com>, which is an international company. You can make $5 to $10 per book.

58 Design and print restaurant menus

A well-designed and presented menu makes a restaurant stand out. You could focus on just menus or create business cards, logo designs and more. Restaurants often require menus to be delivered locally as well as for in the restaurant, so orders won't necessarily be small.

You need to have good graphic design skills and be able to translate what the client has in mind onto paper. You will also need a computer and a good-quality printer.

To get started you could create some menus with a variety of designs to present to restaurants when offering your services. Then visit all the restaurants and cafés in your area outlining what you do and what you charge. Depending on the size of the order and how much work is involved you could make $100 to $200 an order.

59 Produce 'This Is Your Life' DVDs

This style of DVD is usually done for 21st and 50th birthdays, wedding anniversaries and other significant occasions. They can be simply photographs set to music, like a slide show, or they could be snippets of video footage.

The client provides you with what they want, including the selection of songs and photographs, and then you compile it. You can present it on a larger scale where you attend the event with a projector screen and sound equipment, so it becomes a real production rather than just a DVD.

When you begin let all your friends and family know, so word of mouth will spread quickly. Possibly do your first few with a big discount to attract orders.

You can make from $50 per DVD or from $600 if you present it at a venue with the appropriate equipment.

60 Create a niche website

Creating a website about something you love can be a fun way to earn money. The creating isn't the hard part, though. The challenge is getting traffic to your website to generate income. If you have special skills in a particular area of interest, that is a great place to start for your niche website.

All you need is a computer, the right programs, an internet connection and a bit of time to set it up. There are some great websites out there that will help you build your site, so you don't need any prior website knowledge. You can build your website through blogging sites, such as <www.wordpress.org>, or websites such as <www.thesitewizard.com>, which give you a step-by-step guide to everything you need to know.

Great ways to get traffic to your website are by commenting on other websites and blogs and adding a link to yours, discussing your website in forums, as well as letting everyone you know that it exists.

How much you make depends on how you monetise it, which ads you include, how much traffic you get and if you sell products on it. You can make a few hundred to thousands of dollars per month if it is successful.

Design business cards

Designing and printing quality business cards is something you can do from home. Experience in graphic design helps, but if you have an eye for detail and are creative, you will learn the computer side easily.

Create a portfolio of your designs, set up a website and then approach businesses with a special opening offer. You can advertise with flyers directly to businesses, put ads in newspapers or visit businesses personally and show them what you create.

You can charge $200 to $2000 for business cards depending on the quality of materials used to make them, how much work is involved, how many are ordered and how quickly they are needed.

 Complete reference checks for companies

These days businesses outsource as much work as possible to other companies. Small tasks such as reference checks are often not the best use of their time, so it is more beneficial to hire someone else to do it.

Your work would involve checking the applicant's references on their résumés and job applications. You make the calls, do a bit of research and write a summary of what was said, including how the applicant fits the profile being sought and possibly a transcript of the calls.

Businesses could also give you details of what they are looking for and you select the most suitable applicants and screen the rest. This saves businesses a lot of time and — as we all know — time is money.

Once you have set up your business, advertise by email and flyers, and by informing your friends and family about what you are doing.

Your rates will vary depending on the work involved, factoring in such things as how many phone calls you make and so on, but you could easily charge $30 or more an hour or choose to charge per reference check.

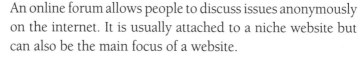
63 Provide online forums

An online forum allows people to discuss issues anonymously on the internet. It is usually attached to a niche website but can also be the main focus of a website.

It's a little involved to set up and it needs to be moderated, but if it's popular you can easily make money from it. Many forums have paid memberships, which is one way you can definitely make money. You can also add Google ads to the website, on various threads (a thread is a discussion), in the sidebars or at the top and bottom of the site.

If your website goes well, you can hire others to moderate the forums for you, which would free up your time.

To get started you will need to build the website that will contain your forum, then start advertising it. You could provide a free offer to get people to join and get your forum known. Linking up with other websites and forums in the same niche will help get like-minded people to your website.

Depending on your website's popularity, you can make thousands of dollars a month from it.

Buy positively geared properties

This may seem impossible, but if you look hard, you can find positively geared properties. A positively geared property is one where the rent received covers the repayments of the property, as well as expenses such as rates and insurance, and you end up making an income from the property.

An easy way to work out if a property is positively geared or not is to divide the house price by 1000 and double the number you are left with. For example, a $350 000 property would need to be rented out for $700 a week. For more information, read Steve McKnight's book *From 0 to 130 Properties in 3.5 Years*.

You are more likely to find a positively geared property by looking at cheaper homes in country towns instead of big homes in the city.

To get started you will need to do lots of research on property, as well as contact your bank to see if it will lend to you, then it is simply a matter of finding the right property. As your portfolio grows your income will, too.

You may start off earning $50 a week, but as your portfolio grows and rent increases you can end up making thousands of dollars a week.

 Buy group homes

Many property investors are interested in buying group homes instead of regular houses they can rent. A group home is just a house but each room is rented individually instead of the whole house. A house that might be rented for $400 a week with four bedrooms can possibly have each room rented for $150 each instead, which becomes $200 more profit.

It can be slightly trickier to manage, but it is an extremely popular housing solution for areas around universities with students. You will need to conduct interviews and pre- and post-rental inspections for each individual renter, which can cause disagreements and problems between the renters.

Many investors prefer this option over regular rentals as the house is never completely empty, and often when someone is moving out, one of the other renters will have someone in mind to move in, which saves on advertising fees.

To advertise your property you can contact the university or other schools near your home. Since there is only so much university housing available, many universities keep records of alternative housing options for students and you should ask to appear on this list.

How much you make will be determined by the property's area, the house and your expenses, but you could make thousands of dollars a year.

  66 Accept deliveries

If you are a stay-at-home parent, you could accept deliveries during the day on other people's behalf for a fee and they could pick them up after work in the evening. Since many people are working longer hours as well as doing shift work, this can be a very useful service. This could also interest those who work nightshift because their sleep would not be interrupted by deliveries throughout the day. There are also many occupations that make it difficult for you to accept deliveries while you are at work.

When you begin send out flyers and tell your friends and family about what you are doing. Those interested can email or call you for details and to arrange for goods to be delivered to you.

You could charge a few dollars per delivery. How much you make a week will vary according to how many packages you accept, but this is an easy way to make a few extra dollars a week if you're at home anyway.

67 Make a dirt bike track

If you have acreage and aren't doing much with it, or even a recreational block, you could consider making a dirt bike track. Basically, people can pay you to ride their dirt bikes in a legal area, as lots of people like riding but have nowhere to do it.

You will have to pay the initial costs to gain council approval, set up tracks, possibly build jumps (but not if you have bumpy land already) and fencing so there is an entry and exit point for payment.

Once you are organised and insured (you will most likely need public liability insurance), let secondary schools, colleges and universities know about your track. Mostly teenage to young adult males will be keen, so target your flyers and advertising to that audience.

You could charge $10 a person per day. If the track is popular, you will begin to make thousands of dollars relatively quickly.

Provide a party house

If you are interested in owning property, a property investment idea is to buy a house for people to use for parties. Many people like the idea of having a big party but either don't have the option because they share a house or don't have the space available, or they don't want to use their own home.

A house that can be hired out for parties would be a great alternative to hiring a hall. You would need to charge a bond and set the home up so it looks lived in. There would also need to be time constraints and rules so you don't upset neighbours and you will probably need to take out public liability insurance as well. You could advertise simply by contacting universities to let their students know about it.

You could charge $500 or more per party, as well as a bond. If the house was hired out both Friday and Saturday nights, you could earn $1000 a week.

Invest in billboards

Billboards are not something that pops to mind when you think about real estate, but they can be a very profitable form of advertising. You can have one placed on your property with council approval or buy one that already exists. They work best on highways or very busy roads.

Businesses then pay to advertise on them. They pay for their signage or you can work the price into a contract. What appears on the billboard is at your discretion.

You can contact your council to see if they are allowable on your land, or look for billboards for sale on real estate websites. Billboards can be rented for $600 to $2500 a month depending on location and size.

70 Offer animal grazing or agisting

If you live on acreage or have vacant land, you could rent the land out for animals to graze. It is up to you which animals you allow. Cattle can really destroy land, so sheep and gentle animals are usually preferable. You will need good fences to contain the animals. You usually charge per head and for legal reasons there are only so many animals you can have in a certain area, so you will need to research thoroughly.

Your agreement should include the amount of rent to be paid, the exact area to be leased, what can be done on the land (for example, whether sheep or cattle can graze), how many animals are allowed, the length of the lease and any maintenance issues (for example, if their animals damage the fences, they need to fix them).

Once you are set up you could advertise in newspapers, such as *The Land,* or self-sufficiency magazines.

How much you make will vary depending on things such as the location and size of your land and how many animals you allow, but you could easily make a few hundred dollars a week on most decent-sized blocks.

71 Rent out your barn

If you live on a rural block or a hobby farm and have a barn, you could hire it out for parties, bush dances and other celebrations. It would need to be cleaner and more presentable than your basic old run-down barn, but it would make a unique location for a wedding reception or a party.

To get the word out you can advertise in newspapers and distribute flyers, or organise for a function to be held in the barn (or hold one yourself) and invite bloggers, journalists, your local newspaper and magazines to come along and write a review. This would be excellent exposure for you.

You can decide how much you rent your barn for, what else you provide, the cost of the bond and so on, but you could easily make in excess of $300 a night.

72 Design blog backgrounds

If you are computer savvy, you could design blog backgrounds as it is fairly easy to learn. You can either make ready-made templates that people can load onto their blogs or you can create custom-designed backgrounds and blog-related features. I know many people who started doing this on the side and then ended up so busy they now do it full-time and have even hired extra staff.

Once you get the hang of designing backgrounds, headers, buttons and other features, each blog background won't take long to complete. And there are so many blogs out there now that you won't be short of business!

Most people advertise from their own blog, which you can set up for free. They then do blog hops and comment on other blogs to attract exposure and customers. You can make $50 to $200 per background depending on what is involved.

73 Design websites

Every business today needs a website. It's the first thing people check when looking at your business. It doesn't need to be huge or have a lot on it, but it is necessary if you want your business to be seen. This is where you come in. Designing an easy-to-use website is not something everyone can do, but is very important.

You can do courses in web design but I know many people who are self-taught. Include your portfolio on your own website, and maybe offer to design a few websites for free or at a heavily discounted rate to appear in your portfolio. Once you are set up you can advertise through friends and family, blogs, websites and social media such as Facebook and Twitter.

You can make a few hundred dollars for a very simple website right up to thousands of dollars for more detailed ones.

74 Create family photograph compilations

Family photograph compilations are great for those families who can't all get together for a family photo. For you to get involved, each family member sends a picture of themselves to one member of the family who then forwards it to you to create a photographic design with all of them in it.

All you need is a computer and a photo editing program. You can provide a photo on its own or as part of a package, including a certain number of prints of different sizes, framed or unframed, on canvas and so on. There are many options for making money this way.

When you are getting started you could set up a stall in a shopping centre to get exposure, contact local family history centres to see if they will recommend you or stock some flyers, or contact schools and offer to do it for fundraising. This would be a great gift for Mother's or Father's Days, for anniversaries and for grandparents as well.

You can charge $100 or more depending on the size of the job, how many prints are selected or the type of package.

Write jokes for magazines

Lots of magazines and newspapers constantly need little jokes to be used as space fillers at the end of articles and some have dedicated jokes pages.

Any time you think of a joke or hear one, write it down and send it to one of these publications. You will find their contact details and terms and conditions on their website and then send in your material according to their instructions. Make sure you include your name and contact details so they can contact you and pay you if they use your joke.

You can make $25 or more per joke. The payment varies from publication to publication, depending on what it is used for.

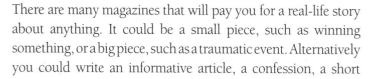

76 Write magazine articles

There are many magazines that will pay you for a real-life story about anything. It could be a small piece, such as winning something, or a big piece, such as a traumatic event. Alternatively you could write an informative article, a confession, a short story or even write up an interview with someone.

There is usually a word limit, which you will need to check with the magazine, and some of them like photos to be included, which may not be returned.

Start by going to different magazine websites to see what they require, then write away. Most accept email contributions, which makes it easier to include photos.

You can make $150 to $3000 or more a story, depending on its length and what it is used for in the magazine.

77 Start a coupon newspaper

Coupons are big in the US and many people wish we had coupons here. You could create a coupon newspaper for your area. Approach businesses and sell advertising space to them in your coupon newspaper. To appear in your newspaper they need to offer customers a discount of some sort.

It is up to you to determine the newspaper's layout, the size and cost of the ads, and how to structure the ads; for example, in beauty, entertainment and home renovation sections. Make all the ads colourful and cheery because you want them to stand out. You will also need to find a suitable printer to print it for you.

You then need to find a way to distribute it. You could do it yourself or through your local catalogue distributor. Contact them for information.

You could make thousands of dollars if your newspaper is done well.

78 Write cartoons, puzzles, tips or product reviews for newspapers and magazines

U18

There are so many things you can write and send to newspapers and magazines. They are constantly seeking miscellaneous fillers such as household and savings tips, product reviews, and puzzles such as crosswords, Sudoku and search-a-words.

All you need to do is sit down and write a few ideas or create some puzzles, then contact the magazines or newspapers you want to send them to. You will need to check what newspapers and magazines are interested in to ensure what you are sending is acceptable.

You can get paid from $25 for a tip and often more like $50 or $100 for a puzzle.

79 Take advantage of bank account opening bonuses

Most banks will offer a bonus to open an account with them. This is not something you could do all the time, but you can keep your eye out and take advantage of the bonuses when they are available.

Often what is being offered is either a sign up bonus for $50 or $100, or it might be a per use bonus where you get paid after using your debit card or transferring money into the account. There are also bonuses available at different times for each service that the banks offer. It doesn't take long to fill out the application and most of it can be done online now. Be aware, though, that every application you make goes on your credit file.

You can often make $25 to $50 for an everyday account, at least $100 for a credit card and $1000 or more to sign up for a home loan.

80 Make YouTube videos

U18

YouTube is a website where people upload videos and you can actually make money on it, too. What you need to do is create a variety of videos and when they get a lot of views you can apply for partnership with YouTube.

Using its partnership you can get a percentage of the money from ads placed alongside your videos. The most important thing before applying for partnership is creating good, popular videos.

Besides the YouTube partnership program, if you have a few popular videos, you could approach businesses that are involved in whatever your video is about to see if they would be interested in sponsoring you either with free products or money in exchange for you mentioning them in your video. It's advertising for them and sponsorship for you.

Many YouTube entrepreneurs are making thousands of dollars but it is entirely dependent on how popular your videos are.

81 Start a mending or alterations business

If you are good at sewing, you could start a mending or alterations business. Offering your services after hours would be very popular as most businesspeople don't have time to organise alterations during work hours. Also if their clothing or uniform gets damaged while at work, they will need it fixed quickly and you could add a surcharge for an emergency service.

All you need is a sewing machine, scissors, cottons and other basic sewing supplies. If you sew, you more than likely already have this equipment.

To attract customers you could approach office workers and offer a discount if they recommend you, distribute flyers around the neighbourhood, approach drycleaners and other businesses to see if they will put a flyer in their window, offer a loyalty card with a discount for every fifth mend, contact schools to see if they will put you in their newsletter and advertise with a sign out the front of your house. You could also contact clothing retailers and ask them to recommend you to their customers if they need alterations for clothing they have just purchased.

You can make hundreds of dollars a week doing mending and alterations, and even thousands of dollars if you are very busy.

82 Do the school run

You have to take your kids to school anyway, so why not offer to take others for a small fee to help cover petrol. For example, if you have a five-seater car but only two children, you could take two more children to school.

Picking the kids up from their home and dropping them off at the end of the day gives parents the peace of mind that their children are getting to and from school safely. It can be cheaper than taking a bus, too.

You would only be able to charge a small amount, such as $10 or $20 a week, depending on how far you travel and if you stay to watch the kids enter the school grounds.

83 Lead a walking bus

Generally, if you live close to your children's primary school, you walk your kids there and back daily. You could walk other kids to school at the same time for a fee and lead a walking 'bus'.

This would appeal to many parents because they may not have the time for it and it means that their kids will get a little exercise. It also gives peace of mind knowing that their children are being supervised as they walk to and from school. And kids would like it because they will get to spend more time with their friends.

Find out which kids live en route to school nearby your home, or even in streets adjacent to where you walk, and offer this service to their parents.

You would need contact numbers for emergencies in case a child hurts themselves, your child is unwell and won't be attending school, or if something is witnessed on the way to school such as a car accident and it upsets the children. This is highly unlikely, but it is handy to have numbers in case anything does happen.

You may want to take out insurance, such as public liability, as you just never know what may happen. You will also need to set some rules, such as be ready at 8.30 am, wear a hat daily and a coat if it is cold. It's also wise to have a back-up plan if it rains. For example, will you drive the kids to school or just walk with umbrellas?

This won't pay a lot and you may only end up with one or two extra kids, but it is a valuable service worth offering. You could charge $5 to $10 per child per week and give discounts for children from the same family.

  ## 84 Organise a food co-op

Buying food in bulk often presents itself with significant savings. Since you're already buying food, it's not that hard to buy it in bulk and split it with other people.

You could organise seasonal boxes, where everyone pays $50 and you supply fresh produce in season equal to that amount. Alternatively, you could offer a variety box containing whatever is cheap at the markets or whatever is available for the best deal when you make your purchase.

You can charge the regular per-kilogram price, or a price between the discount you are able to negotiate for buying in bulk and the real price. It's your choice.

You will need to decide things like if you will be dropping off the produce or if your customers pick up from you; do they pay before you shop or when they pick up; and will you offer the service weekly, fortnightly or monthly?

You can charge a fee for your time and the petrol used or include your costs as part of an admin fee. Since it's you who does the buying, you can often get extra items for free and make enough to cover your produce with money to spare. Ideally food co-ops are made up of 12 to 28 families. The more families the larger the discounts, but the more work is involved in purchasing and sorting goods.

Check with family and friends first, then ask around your neighbourhood to see who would be interested to join. Make sure you get money upfront to ensure all costs are covered.

Depending on how often you do it, how many families are involved and the discounts you pass on, you can earn anything from $50 per week for doing your own shopping!

85 Shop for others

Shopping for others was more popular before stores started offering online shopping and home deliveries, but not all shops offer these services and often items on sale in store are more expensive online, so it can work out cheaper for someone like you to shop for other people's groceries.

You can charge either a fee to do it or a percentage of the shopping total. Simply take your clients' lists with you when you do your shopping and deliver it when you are done. You can offer additional services, such as visiting speciality shops or the chemist, depending on your clients' needs and the time you have.

Set aside a time each week, fortnight or month to do the shopping. Arrange to receive the money when you pick up their lists to ensure you are paid. If they are purchasing the same things each time, they will have a good idea of how much things cost.

You can make $25 to $50 per week for just a bit of extra time added to your usual shopping trip.

86 Advertise with car wrap

If you drive around a fair bit, have a reasonably modern car that is well looked after and you drive well, you could offer businesses to advertise with signage on your car. They pay for the signage to be made and pay you a fee to advertise their business for a set period.

You will need to keep your car clean at all times and possibly be required to do a certain amount of driving. This is a moving advertisement for them and can work out cheaper than running a regular ad in the paper.

Some businesses prefer full wraparound advertising where your entire car is covered in signage, while others just want advertising on your rear window.

You will need to discuss things such as what happens if you have a car accident, does their insurance cover the cost if you need to redo the advertising, will they remove the signage at the end of the agreed time or do you need to pay for that to be done, and will they pay for weekly car cleaning to keep it in perfect condition? Ask lots of questions and confirm everything in writing.

Depending on how long you do it and how much driving is done, you can make from $50 a week providing the business pays to put the signage on and remove it.

87 Be a mystery shopper

If you are a mystery shopper, you literally get paid to shop, do your banking, eat dinner in restaurants, stay at hotels, fly interstate and even use theme parks. However, not all mystery shopping companies deal in all of these options; some might be for take-away food or coffee, while others cover everything.

Once you have signed up with a mystery shopping company you will receive emails informing you when shops are available in your area, but this is not a guarantee of work. You then need to log into its website and click on the shop you would like to 'do'. The assignment — for example, where you are shopping, what you should buy and the amount you will be paid — is all there for you to read and decide if you would like to do it.

You need to be very observant when doing the shop. It sometimes helps to take notes, but you can't be obvious about it as you mustn't blow your cover.

Work is available for pretty much anywhere, so accept the jobs that suit your lifestyle. For example, you can get paid to deposit money into your own bank account or to do your groceries. Once you have a bit of experience you can then get bigger assignments, such as taking flights and using accommodation.

The shopping is the fun part. When you have completed a shop at the set time and day you then need to log into your mystery shopping account and fill out a survey about your shop. These can be quite long and the companies are very particular about spelling and grammar, so you need to give good, clear and accurate descriptions of everything that occurred.

There are sample surveys and help sheets for you to view before committing to your first shop. After you have done them a few times you'll know what to expect and the surveys will be easier and faster to fill out.

To get started check out <www.hoedshopper.com.au> and <www.shopangels.com.au>.

You usually have to pay for the services upfront, then be reimbursed by the mystery shopping company for the amount you spent, plus an amount for actually completing the shop. Some mystery shopping assignments pay as little as $5 while others pay more than $50.

 ## 88 Become a party planner

All party plan companies have different policies, including how many parties you need to organise, whether you can only be a member of one or many party plans and how many meetings you need to attend.

There are pros and cons to this type of work. You need to have confidence in the product and be comfortable to stand in front of strangers describing your product. Some companies will require to you do parties to pay off your kit, while others just get you to buy the kit. You will need to do the required training when you begin and you'll probably have to report to someone about your sales and parties each week. You will also need to be able to travel.

For a list of various party plans you can join, check <www.partyplans.com.au>.

If you would like to work your way up, you can get a car and even receive a salary instead of just a percentage of party sales. By doing two to three parties a week with a $600 sale average, you could make $300 to $800. Many companies also give bonuses for reaching various sales goals, and the rewards are sometimes cash, appliances, vouchers and bedding rather than always more product.

89 Buy and sell cars

This is only possible if you know what you are doing. If you are a mechanic or panel beater and can fix cars cheaply, this is a great option. Or if you live in a location where cars are expensive but regularly travel where they are sold more cheaply, you could always buy them and drive them home and sell them.

Another option if you are already renting cars to backpackers, is to sell your cars to them so they can drive around in their own car and offer to buy the cars back from them at the end of their trip at a heavily reduced price, such as $500. It saves the backpackers trying to sell their cars and then you can resell them.

You can make thousands of dollars doing this, but only if you know what you are doing. If you don't, it will just end up costing you thousands of dollars.

90 Set up signs for real estate agents

Many agents rush from one open home inspection to the other and many now pay someone else to set up and pack up their signage. It won't take you long. You just need to drive around a few suburbs and put up the signs where they want, then take them down when required and return them a few hours later.

Alternatively, some agents prefer all the signs to be put up in the morning and taken down that evening, so it could be done alongside the rest of your other daily activities.

The pay varies depending on the area you live in and how many open home inspections are scheduled but you could make in excess of $50 for what is essentially easy work.

91 Become a property developer

Property development has worked really well for some and really badly for others. You do need a bit of money to start, but many investment clubs or groups of people are doing this together, making it easier to arrange the money and get loans, and make money faster.

You could buy a block of land and build units or townhouses on it, or buy pre-existing ones and renovate them to sell off.

Once you have selected what you plan to do, most of the work can be organised from your own home, such as arranging quotes, organising tradesmen and filling out forms.

There are loads of variables for how much you will end up making from property development—if it goes well, you could make hundreds of thousands of dollars.

Redevelop a motel into offices or apartments

If an old motel is located near shops or there are shops going to be built near an old motel, it is worth more as office space or studio apartments than as a motel. If you're lucky, you might not have to do much besides change the title to be able to sell it. Most motel rooms are already studio apartments with a kitchenette and ensuite. You will need to check with your council for approval and you will need some money to buy it, but this could be a very lucrative option.

You will only need to renovate part of the building before renting it out or selling the rooms. Depending on how much work needs to be done to the rest of the building, you may find you can do it outside business hours, which will make it easier to rent or sell the offices.

The amount you will get will vary greatly but you could easily make $100 000 or more in most areas.

Rent a holiday house

This is an alternative to a normal rental property. It is not necessarily one for yourself, but a home in a tourist or holiday destination that is leased at peak periods, and usually leased for five or more times the price than if leased weekly. There can be a lot of management costs, unless you are able to do it yourself, which will eat into your profit.

Keep in mind that the house may be vacant for a period over the winter months if it is a beach location or over summer if it is near a ski resort.

Depending on the location, the style and condition of the house, management costs and other variables, you could make $200 or more a week.

94 Create a local real estate website

There are lots of real estate websites, but ones that specifically focus on certain areas are not as common. However, they tend to be easier to use and more popular for their particular areas than the big real estate websites. They usually provide more localised information, which makes them easier to research an area.

It is not expensive to set up a website like this if you know what you are doing. Domain names can be purchased for under $10 a year. It is the advertising and attracting people to your website that will be more expensive.

If done well, you could make thousands of dollars a week by featuring property listings and ads in sidebars, as well as commissions if you choose this option as well.

95 Become a freelance journalist

Instead of being employed by a particular magazine you could write articles on current events, fashion or whatever subject you like and submit them to various magazines. The income is more irregular than being employed full-time but you have the freedom to choose what you write about and have more options about where your work is published than if you were employed by a single magazine. It is also something you can do after hours if you are working full time, or it can be done from home if you have a family.

The publication rates for stories varies a lot from a few hundred dollars to a few thousand dollars, depending on what you are writing about, who publishes it and how well you are known.

96 Sell your gold

There are little kiosks popping up everywhere that pay cash for your broken gold jewellery. Be aware that what you get for your gold is a miniscule amount compared with what it is actually worth. There are also online gold buyers that offer a slightly higher price, such as <www.goldcompany.com.au>.

How much you get depends on how pure the gold is (for example, 9 carat, 18 carat, 24 carat), how heavy the piece is and how much the price of gold is that day. You do not get paid for any stones set in the jewellery, even though they are taken with the gold, so you are better off removing any stones and selling them separately.

If your pieces aren't broken, you should try selling them through other methods such as online with eBay or through newspaper classifieds.

Depending on the price of gold on the day you could make around $2 a gram by selling to a gold buyer, or more if you are selling whole pieces such as rings privately.

 97 Sell second–hand CDs and DVDs

If you have any CDs and DVDs lying around, you could sell them online or to second-hand dealers. People are always on the lookout for rare copies, so you never know your luck. You could also offer to sell your friends' CDs and DVDs for them and get a percentage of the sale. Many people can't be bothered doing this themselves, so it could end up quite profitable for you. However, your CDs and DVDs need to be in good condition with no scratches.

You can contact your local second-hand CD and DVD store to see what you can get for your copies, or you could check how much they sell for online at websites such as <www.fishpond. com.au>. To do this, look up the item you wish to sell, click on it if it's in stock, then click on the 'sell yours' link.

By selling online you could make between $3 and $20 depending on how rare or sought after the item is. From a second-hand store you would be lucky to get $1 or slightly more per item.

98 Deliver flyers and catalogues

The pay for doing a paper route isn't great, but there are ways to make it easier for yourself. Many people deliver flyers and catalogues because you are essentially getting paid to exercise instead of paying to go to the gym.

Distributing newspapers pays more than delivering individual flyers and you only need to fold one item. If you get a lot of flyers to deliver that need to be done together, the pay is higher but there will be a lot of folding. Since this is something you can do while pushing your kids in a pram, it can easily be done by stay-at-home parents.

To get started look in your local newspaper for ads looking for catalogue deliverers or contact the businesses in the catalogues to see who they distribute through.

You will usually make $50 to $100 a week, depending on the size of your area, how many areas you do and how much you have to deliver.

99 Sell second-hand books

If you know what you are looking for, you can make a fair bit from selling second-hand books. You can purchase them cheaply at garage sales and second-hand shops and then resell them to second-hand bookshops, online or do a market stall.

Most popular novels do not sell well second-hand. Finance books, text books and nonfiction books all sell better than most fiction, though there is some sought-after fiction. I once bought a book for $25 and resold it for $85, so if you do your research you can find some really worthwhile books.

You can sell books on websites such as <www.ebay.com.au>, <www.gumtree.com.au> or <www.fishpond.com.au>. Items on Fishpond stay listed until they sell and there is no charge to list an item but it can take a while to sell them and not all books appear on the site. To check if the book you want to sell is listed, simply look it up and if it's there, select the 'sell yours' button.

You can make $2 to in excess of $100 per book depending on rarity and value.

 ## 100 Arrange parcel forwarding

A lot of businesses do not post overseas. For a fee you could set up a website where packages can be sent to you and then you send it on to whomever it is overseas who purchased it. There are many items that can only be bought in Australia but are extremely popular overseas and vice versa.

By living in Australia and offering an address that people can send their orders to enables overseas customers to buy what they like from Australia and you ship it to them. They pay all costs and an extra fee to you.

To gather information about costs contact reputable international couriers for their fees, as well as Australia Post for its postal fees. Then set up your website and advertise it.

You can charge around $10 or slightly more per package.

101 Offer a break-up resell service

When people break up they do not usually want to deal with the things their ex partner gave them or items that remind them of their ex. You could sell items people received from their ex for a percentage of the sale. This also allows people to get around the guilt of selling an item, as they are not technically selling it—they are employing someone to do it for them.

Jewellery, books, CDs, anything that reminds them of their ex could be sold by you for either a set fee or a percentage of the sale. However, you will need them to sign something verifying that the items are in fact theirs to sell and they are not selling off someone else's property.

To get started you could offer your services to friends and family or contact counselling offices to see if they will recommend your services.

You can get from $50 a client, depending on what is being sold, the number of items and other variables.

102 Collect cans for cash

Collecting cans for cash does not pay a lot and collection points are not always easy to locate, but it is something anyone can do. Some outlets also accept plastic bottles, which are sometimes worth more.

Collecting cans is easy. You can look out for them during your walks and they are easy to locate at parks, bus stops, beaches, and around local shops and restaurants. You can ask friends or neighbours to keep their cans for you, too.

It may take a while to collect enough cans to earn decent money, but if you find them during your regular daily activities, it can be a way to make routine tasks profitable.

Firstly find out where you can cash in the cans in your local area and their operating hours. Then you just need to collect cans and cash them in.

The usual rate is 5 cents a can, so you would need to collect 100 cans to get $5.

103 sell firewood

If you have a large block of land with trees that have been cleared, you could sell the wood as firewood. Even if you do not have your own block of land where you can grow and cut trees, you can still sell firewood. Arrange a deal with a tree surgeon for trees that have been cut down to be delivered to you or for you to pick up. You give them a referral fee and then sell the wood, or give them a percentage of each sale from their wood.

You could contact local petrol stations and independent supermarkets to see if you can sell the wood there, as well as advertise the service by distributing flyers or putting a sign outside your house.

It is a bit of work to collect the wood, cut it and possibly deliver it (for an extra fee), but you can make a few hundred dollars per tree.

104 Sell second-hand computer games

Most technology is not worth selling second-hand, but some consoles, such as Nintendo 64 and Super Nintendo, and old school games are actually highly sought after, despite being years old. If you have a quick search online for the going prices, you will know what to keep an eye out for.

You can find these games and their consoles at garage sales, by checking classifieds and sometimes online, where you can buy them cheaply and resell for more.

Some games will sell for $50 or more on their own but you can easily make over $500 for a console with some popular games.

105 Try metal detecting

You won't find any buried treasure and more than likely you will only find 20 cents here and there, but metal detecting can be a fun pastime. It can be a fun activity to do with your kids during walks or when you're at the beach and it can be a profitable venture.

Many people also use metal detecting when collecting cans to sell, and when looking for metals such as copper or jewellery. Legally jewellery or items of significant worth must be handed to the police so they can try to locate the owner, but if an item isn't claimed you can keep it.

You can find items worth $5 or more a week by metal detecting in parks, at beaches and during your general walks.

106 Be a dumpster diver

Dumpster diving sounds disgusting but it is becoming quite a pastime, even a lifestyle for many people. If you live near schools with dorms on campus or in an area where many young people move in and out, you will be able to pick times they will be clearing out their things in preparation for moving and you're likely to find some great things that you can sell.

Your success will vary a lot depending on when you do it and the time you can devote to it, your yuk factor (how dirty are you willing to get) and what you actually find.

You will probably only make $10 here and there but you might find the odd thing worth $100 or more.

107 Collect and resell golf balls

If you live near a golf course, you could walk around it daily and collect stray golf balls. If you ask the owner, you may get permission at the end of the day to go over the golf course looking for stray balls. If they don't want you to resell them, they might pay you to collect the balls at the end of the day and give them back to the club.

For those you find and can keep, you can then sell in groups of five for a few dollars. This is something even kids could do and they would have fun doing it.

Depending on how many golf balls you find and how many you sell, you could make from $10 a week.

108 Sell items on eBay for others

Many people like the idea of selling on eBay but have no idea how to do it or are just put off by the process. However, the more you do it, the easier it is to sell things as many buyers are wary of first-time sellers and you'll have much more success with a high feedback score.

You could offer to sell items for people for a set fee or for a percentage of the sale. You would need to be clear that there is no guarantee that their items will sell, but if the items are popular there is a good chance they will. You also need to decide whether there are items you don't want to sell and whether your clients pay a set amount upfront and then the rest when/if the item sells. Make sure you work all of these things out at the start so you don't end up out of pocket.

Depending on how much you sell and how much you charge, you could make from $50 a client.

109 Design and make fishing lures

Lures are designed to imitate live bait, making it easier to catch other fish. They come in a variety of types depending on their purpose. Some are easy to make, while others are more complex.

To do this you need to be a bit handy, but it is easy to find designs online that you can make and sell. It's best to try the different designs personally to see the varied levels of success and to make sure you know what you are talking about when trying to sell them.

You could try selling them online, to local fishing equipment shops, or even down at beaches and wharves where you'll find people fishing. Your profit will probably be $2 to $3 a lure.

1 1 0 Buy properties to renovate and sell

There is a lot of work involved in buying properties to renovate and sell, but many people have done it successfully. You need to do a lot of research before you begin as you want to buy the right property in the right location so you don't have to do to much to make a profit.

Many people overlook this idea because buying property in capital cities has become so expensive, but it can still be done without paying a fortune in outlying areas. And if you buy and renovate a few homes in the outer areas to begin with, you will soon be able to afford more expensive and more profitable homes in capital cities.

To get started you will need to contact your bank and work out your finances to see if it is doable for you. Next you will need to research property in the area that you want to buy in, as well as the cost of renovations. Then it is simply a matter of finding a suitable property, buying it, fixing it and selling it.

There are many variables involved but you can make $50 000 or much more for each home.

111 Become a movie critic

This is not as easy as many people assume it to be. You do get paid to watch movies and write what you think about them, but you don't get to just watch the movies you like—you have to watch all types of movies.

It is not always an easy area to get into, but if you are good, you can write reviews for magazines, newspapers, radio stations, websites and more.

You could always start your own website or blog reviewing movies as well. Posting reviews on blogs and even on YouTube will be the fastest and easiest way to get started as you can build your reputation while still trying to crack mainstream media.

Many freelance movie critics are paid $1 a word or less for a review.

112 Make money from liquidation sales

There are a couple of ways you can make money from liquidation sales—either host them or go to them, buy up and resell elsewhere. They are held at various times and you never know what is going to be there. If you stick to an area of speciality, you are much better off than just going there to buy anything because it is cheap.

Some are advertised on TV and radio, otherwise there are websites you can check. They are usually held at the same places each year, which makes it easier to track them down and plan which ones you want to go to.

Once you know what to buy, how much to pay and where the sales are located, you just need to go and buy what you want to sell. You can resell things online on <www.ebay.com.au> or <www.oztion.com.au>, or even through your local classifieds.

Depending on how much you spend and resell, you could make $50 or $500 or more.

Part II

MAKE MONEY
FROM YOU

This section covers a variety of ways you can make money using just yourself. Most of the ideas are not ways to make a regular income but they can provide a significant boost in income when you put them into action.

1 1 3   Sell your hair

Human hair is popular to use for hair extensions and for wig making as it can be styled and coloured like regular hair. Even if you think no-one would want your hair because it is a common colour, they do. Plain browns are actually excellent bases for colour matching (dying hair to match any colour). There are a few things you will need to take into consideration:

⇨ Untreated hair is more favourable and will fetch a better price. So no perms, dyes or bleaching.

⇨ The healthier the hair, the higher the price you will get. You hair will be in better condition if you are a nonsmoker, don't use drugs and live a healthy lifestyle.

⇨ Your hair needs to be 25 centimetres to 30 centimetres long at least and in good condition. Long continuous pieces of hair are needed for extensions and hair pieces.

⇨ Find a buyer before you cut your hair. There are a few websites out there specialising in hair sales.

⇨ When you cut your hair arrange it into a low pony tail or braid first.

For more information go to <http://sellyourhairaustralia.com.au>. You could earn upwards of $500 for selling your hair.

1 1 4   Undergo medical experiments

There are lots of companies who will pay you to be a part of their medical trials. Some are as easy as completing sleep research or quit smoking programs; others can have side effects, so choose wisely. While some research companies only pay by supplying the medicine that they are testing, others will pay you a fee, plus pay for accommodation and meals for the duration of the tests.

You will find many of these jobs advertised in newspapers, online, on university and college noticeboards, and occasionally on radio. Thoroughly check the company you will be doing research for before you begin. Is it reputable? Has it done many of these medical trials before? What is written into the waiver? What happens if there are side effects—do they provide your treatment or pay for you to be treated elsewhere if necessary?

Some trials seek healthy participants, while others require you to have certain medical issues or addictions. These may be as simple as constant hay fever right through to more serious afflictions, such as cancer or smoking addictions. Sometimes you will need to get confirmation from your doctor that you are fit (or ill) to undergo the medical trial before it can commence.

If you are interested, contact the international company Paid Clinical Trials <www.paidclinicaltrials.org/dir/location/australia>. The usual daily rate you will be paid is $100 to $300.

 115 Undergo psychological research

Much like undergoing medical research, psychological research is varied and doesn't provide a constant stream of income. It typically involves filling out surveys and answering questions; nothing terribly hard, though it can make you re-evaluate aspects of your life. It's advertised in much the same way as for medical research.

Some psychological research will require you to complete blood tests and full medical examinations, but these are carried out by the professionals doing the research and will not cost you extra.

Applicants usually need to have a medically diagnosed psychological condition as the research will involve gathering data and possibly testing new therapies and treatments. Sometimes companies seek children for these tests, usually from the ages of six to 17 years. It is up to you if you feel comfortable about having your children tested.

For paid psychological research jobs search career websites such as <www.jobsearch.com.au>. You will usually be paid between $100 and $300 a day.

116 Work as a dating escort

There are agencies that require dating escorts for people and that is as far as it goes. Your clients will most often be businessmen who are simply too busy for a romantic life. They hire dates to attend business functions with them; however, you need to thoroughly research an agency to ensure that it is only a date that is required.

Not everyone can do it. Following are a few requirements:

➢ You need to be attractive and take care of yourself. Age is not as important as presentation.

> You must have confidence. You will be going to events where you won't know anyone and you will be expected to behave in a certain manner.

> Dress well. Many business functions are full of Ralph Lauren suits; you will need to dress accordingly.

> Be well spoken and knowledgeable about current events.

For this type of work you can usually earn about $60 an hour plus free dinner and drinks. Dates are often a two-hour minimum but are frequently three hours or more.

117 Become a model

Models are needed in all shapes and sizes. There is a surprising amount of work for mums sized 8 to 12.

The first thing you will need to do is find a good reputable agency. They will arrange for a portfolio to be made and possibly some classes in grooming and deportment and catwalk training. Research the agency thoroughly. There are many unscrupulous agencies out there who are only interested in taking money from you and not actually setting you up with any work.

Carefully check any contract you are asked to sign, in particular the fees and commissions and what is required of you. For example, some agencies may not let you dye or cut your hair, or gain or lose five kilograms. Some contracts can be very strict, others more flexible.

If the agency is confident it will find you work, ask if any upfront costs can be deducted from your first job. Once the contracts are complete you will be informed about when you need to attend casting auditions. These are not paid but are opportunities to try out for modelling jobs.

If you are interested in becoming a model, Chadwicks <www.chadwickmodels.com> is a reputable agency, or for plus-size modelling check out <www.bgmmodels.com.au>.

You can earn anywhere from $250 to thousands of dollars for each modelling job.

118 Work as a TV or movie extra

This type of work is best if you live in a major city, where things actually get filmed. You can pick up a fair amount of work, but it is varied and not reliable income. However, if you are extremely lucky, you may get a more regular extra position on a soap or TV drama.

Many extras are paid $50 to $250 a shoot. A shoot can take anything from half an hour to the entire day. And a day can be eight to 12 hours long, which doesn't make for the best hourly rate.

Agencies are often looking for a wide variety of people, so there aren't usually any height or weight restrictions. You just need to be regularly available. Many modelling agencies also need extras, so if you are considering either modelling or working as a TV extra, you may as well go for both.

Besides contacting agencies directly, such as StarNow <www.starnow.com.au>, you will sometimes find ads in newspapers or online seeking extras, but this is rare.

You can do a quick search to check the reputation of many agencies. Reputable agencies usually don't ask for large upfront fees, so that will often be a warning sign of a dodgy agency.

As an extra you can expect to earn an average of $100 a day.

119 Become an art model

Art schools and classes usually advertise in newspapers or on community noticeboards for art models, which usually require you to model nude. The pay isn't usually very much, but the work can be interesting and enjoyable.

Once you have found a job you will need to discuss details, such as payment, how long the session will go for, how many breaks you will get, how many poses you will be doing and any other questions you might have.

There are a few things you will want to take to the job. Pack a towel to sit on, water, lunch and snacks if it is a long session, a robe to wear during breaks and a timer so you know when to change poses.

To find work contact your local art school or community centre offering life drawing courses to see if they are looking for models. Nude models usually get paid $25 to $50 an hour, although some are paid upwards of $200. Sessions can last one, three or more hours.

120 Work as a spruiker

You know those people who stand at the front of stores talking into a microphone all day about the 'Great deals inside!'? Well, not many people want to do this, so you can actually get a fair amount of work as a spruiker. You just need to speak clearly and have a lot of confidence, and you will spend most of your time talking into a microphone and getting ignored.

You will be required to stand for anywhere from one hour to the entire day. It can be a hard job, constantly on your feet, trying to think of things to say to lure people into the store you are spruiking for.

You need to be well presented, with styled hair and make-up (if you're female), manicured nails, polished shoes and usually wearing business attire. It helps to have a bottle of water nearby as talking for long periods will make your mouth dry.

Many modelling and entertainment agencies also offer spruiking services, so contact those in your area. If there are shops in your area that use spruiking services, you could ask which agency they use and contact it. Alternatively, approach businesses directly to offer your services. Spruikers typically earn $50 an hour and work three-hour shifts.

121 Become a hand or foot model

Jewellery catalogues often require hand models. To do this work your hands need to be attractive, in excellent condition, moisturised and manicured. Many hand models wear gloves all the time and don't do anything that might damage their hands, which can be tricky.

To get started take some photos of your hands in various poses. Check magazines and ads for inspiration. You don't need professionally taken photos, they just need to look attractive.

Once you have a good selection of photos contact a modelling agency to enquire about being a hand model. They may not have any vacancies on their books, so arrange a time to call back.

Professional hand models are not always used for advertisements. Sometimes staff members are used because they are cheaper and it can be more convenient. The work is sparse, but if you have truly beautiful hands, this is something you can do to make money.

Most hand models make $35 to $50 an hour or are paid a few hundred dollars per shoot.

122 Work as a body extra

Not all actors like to get naked for their movies or TV shows, so you can make a bit by being a body double for them. It is usually through a modelling or talent agency that you will get work.

Generally you need to be fit, toned and in good shape — remember, your body is giving the illusion that the actor is perfect! Your body needs to be free of scars, stretch marks, tattoos and piercings. If the actor you are going to work as a double for has any of these physical characteristics, they can be applied by the make-up department so it is better if you are a clean canvas.

Your lifestyle may be restricted because your physical appearance needs to remain the same constantly. No gaining a bit of weight here or losing a bit there. You will be hired for what you look like right now and need to maintain that appearance.

For a short shift with no nudity you can earn $150, while longer shifts pay more like $800. If you are doing any nudity, you can earn double that amount.

123 Work as a lookalike

If you're always getting told that you look like someone famous, there are actually agencies that will get you work at parties and events impersonating the celebrity. It can be a very competitive industry though, and many people have undergone surgery to look like their chosen celebrity. You also need to dress like them, which can get very expensive.

Being a lookalike is more than just looking like a celebrity. You need to act and talk like them. Whoever you choose to be, you need to hone in on their unique characteristics. What do they do that makes them stand out or that gets noticed by the public? Little gestures add up and perfecting them will make you a more valuable lookalike.

The pay varies greatly, but sometimes if you are the only lookalike for your celebrity you can secure travel and accommodation expenses as well.

Depending on who you impersonate, their popularity and how many similar lookalikes there are in your area, you can make between $500 and $1000 a night. The pay increases for very famous celebrities and for being more than just a lookalike, which is why you should perfect your celebrity's mannerisms.

1 2 4 Enter impersonator competitions

Another option if you look like a famous celebrity is to enter lookalike competitions and win cash prizes. It's not regular money and you need to constantly be looking online, in newspapers, and on TV and radio for the competitions, but the prizes can be awesome. And it can provide great exposure if you are just starting to work as a lookalike.

However, just because you and your friends think you are the best impersonator doesn't mean you will win. Much of it has to do with how well you connect with the audience and the judges as a performer, so the more charismatic you are the better your chances of winning.

Winners of lookalike competitions often receive $10 000 to $20 000 in cash prizes as well as contracts for work. Runners-up usually secure $2000 to $5000 each. You will also get lots of exposure and will be in a position to charge more if you want professional work as a lookalike.

1 2 5 Become a children's party entertainer

A clown, a fairy, a pirate, whatever you fancy, you could dress up and perform at children's parties. It can be quite exhausting, but if you love kids, it can be very rewarding.

Just choose the character you would like to be and how you will run the parties. What games will be played? Do you just provide entertainment or do you offer goody bags? Will you sing and dance or do magic tricks? Will you do crafts with the kids so they get to take something home?

You can charge in excess of $75 depending on how long you entertain for and what you do. Children's parties are usually short, so you can do a few in a day.

126 Work as a hired friend

Not everyone is the life of the party. Some people need help to get an event started or to keep it going. Others just like to look as though they have more friends than they really do.

If you are charismatic, love being the centre of attention, tell good jokes and are easy to get along with and entertaining, you could be hired to liven up parties or get them started.

A good way to start is by word of mouth. You don't really want your face everywhere because people will see you as the hired friend at parties, so you need to be discreet about your work.

Payment varies depending on the length of the event but, on average, you could make in excess of $200 a night plus free drinks and food.

127 Do face painting

Face painting is extremely popular with children and it's a great way to entertain them. Most school fetes and festivals hire face painters for the day, and many shopping centres hire them during school holidays to paint kids' faces too. If you are a children's entertainer, you can add it to your repertoire.

You will need to purchase face painting supplies and work out how much you will charge—usually only a few dollars a face.

To get started contact shopping centres for a school holiday booking or try party entertainment businesses, such as jumping castle hire, to see if they will cross-promote you.

You can make over $50 for an hour or two, even more at school fetes and festivals or if hired by a business or shopping centre.

128 make balloon animals

Making balloon animals is easy to learn and very popular with kids, especially at children's parties. It can be done wherever kids need entertaining, such as school fetes, festivals or markets, or you could try busking. You can buy kits with the right balloons and a pump, and learn how to do it yourself.

You will need to make a variety of animals and shapes. Dogs, flowers and hats seem to be the most popular, but the more you can do the more appealing you will be.

You will only make $1 to $2 per balloon, but you can earn quite a bit in an hour depending on how fast you are.

Part III

MAKE MONEY

SEASONALLY

There are certain times of the year when you can make extra money related to the seasons, religious holidays or celebrations. For example, in November and December during the lead-up to Christmas there are many services you can provide as well as ornaments and gifts that you can make and sell. The same applies to occasions such as Halloween, which is becoming more popular in this country. During other times of the year the changes in the weather present even more opportunities to make money, for example shovelling snow in winter and cooling down with ice in summer.

129 Grow and sell Christmas trees

You will need a bit of space to plant and grow the trees. It can take quite some time for the trees to be large enough to sell, so this is not an instant money maker, but leading up to Christmas real trees are very popular.

You can sell them from your property or wherever they are being grown, at petrol stations, markets or on consignment with various stores.

Prices for real trees start at $40. How much you make will depend on how many you have available, their initial cost, how much they cost to maintain and how many you sell.

130 Install outdoor Christmas lights

Lots of people love the look, but hate actually putting them up. You will need a ladder and a few bits of equipment, but if you already have them, it could cost you nothing to set up. Installing Christmas lights is generally a matter of placing them on a person's roof and around their home. You might also offer to put up other decorations to be displayed outside the house.

Once you get a bit of experience it will become very quick to do. For most people it will be much simpler to pay you to do it rather than spend hours doing it themselves.

You will need specific insurance to cover both yourself in case of injury and your client's property as you don't want to short circuit someone's electricity and be up for a lot of damages.

You could make in excess of $100 per house.

131 Make and sell Christmas puddings

Real, traditional steamed Christmas puddings like grand-mothers used to make take a bit of preparation and very few people have the time to do it. A real homemade pudding tastes divine and pretty much sells itself.

You can sell them at markets or school fairs, or take orders through friends and families and their workmates. You could also offer them as a business fundraiser and donate a portion to their social club fund or Christmas party.

A 500 gram pudding typically sells from $25. How much you make will depend on the size of the puddings, the cost of ingredients and how many you sell.

132 Make and sell Christmas ornaments

One year I made felt Santa bags and candy cane reindeer to sell at markets. The bags sold for $6 and the candy cane reindeer for $1 each. They didn't take long to make and all the materials to make them were cheap.

There are lots of different decorations you can make that don't need to cost a lot, but will definitely sell well if they are cute and unique. Besides markets you could also sell them to your friends and family and their workmates, through your children's school or kinder, or even online if you have your own blog or website. You can expect to make $1 to $2 from each decoration.

133   Design and create Christmas stockings

Unique Christmas stockings make a great gift and can be simple to make. If you can sew, you could create your own designs or use a pattern. They don't need to be made out of Christmas fabric to be Christmassy either.

You could make personalised ones, with the person in mind's interests incorporated into the design or you could feature their names on the stocking. They won't take long to make and can be sold online, at markets or possibly on consignment with shops.

Depending on the cost of materials you could make from $10 per stocking.

134   Make outdoor Christmas displays and decorations

Making unique wooden Christmas decorations such as nativity scenes or scenes from cartoons is not easy. You need to be skilled in both woodwork and painting, and you will need tools and a workspace.

These items are very popular, though, especially reindeers and Santa in his sleigh. Having a few designs will give people something to choose from, but also cuts down your work because you will get faster by making the same designs.

The best way to sell them will be from your home with a sign out the front listing the designs and prices, especially if you live on a busy street.

You can make from $50 for smaller decorations and in excess of $200 for larger ones, such as a sleigh on a rooftop.

135 Put up and decorate Christmas trees

As crazy as it sounds many people like the look of Christmas trees but just do not want to put them up themselves. Or they want the decorations to appear in a more orderly manner and can't seem to place them evenly on the tree.

It is not hard work and you can make a bit from this work. You can do it outside business hours, which makes it easier to do around your regular job or if you're looking after children.

Make a flyer and do a letterbox drop. You can also display the flyer on community noticeboards. If you're lucky, you will get repeat customers each year.

You can expect to make around $25 per tree.

136 Grow and sell orange pumpkins for Halloween

Orange pumpkins can sell for $25 around Halloween, which is a lot for a pumpkin. If you can source the seeds, they are very easy to produce and will grow pretty much wild in a backyard. The seeds are not expensive and you can get lots of pumpkins from just a few seeds.

You can then sell the pumpkins from your home or your workplace and at markets, or you could send an email to friends and family to see if they are interested and if they can spread the word.

Even if you sell 10 pumpkins for $10 each you will earn $100. You could sell them for much higher, though.

137 Create and sell gruesome Halloween treats

There are lots of normal food that can be turned into gruesome treats for Halloween, such as crooked finger cookies and eyeball truffles. They are easy to make and great for those hosting Halloween celebrations or for people to give out to trick or treaters.

You can search for recipes online or just think outside the box to turn your favourite treats into gruesome and grizzly delights. Check your state for health regulations regarding home cooking.

Besides selling them to friends, family and neighbours, they can be sold at markets, or contact local cafes to see if they are interested in selling them, or even try hairdressers and similar businesses to see if they want to buy them to serve with clients' coffees on the day.

You can make a few hundred dollars from selling these at a market stall leading up to Halloween.

138 Accompany trick or treat groups

Halloween is becoming more popular in Australia every year. Many kids want to go trick or treating but most parents either don't have the time or don't want to do it, but at the same time they don't want to let their kids go knocking on strangers' doors.

You could arrange to take groups of kids around the neighbourhoods for a fee. You could take half-hour tours, which would need to be prebooked. It is up to you to prearrange with the neighbours that you visit for the kids to receive lollies or if you leave it to luck.

You could charge from $5 per child. If you take a group of 10, that's $50 for half an hour's work. Of course, you could take more than one group depending on your time available.

1 3 9 Turn your home into a haunted house

During Halloween you could set up your home as a haunted house and charge an admission fee. Decorate each room in a scary way, possibly with a different theme for each room, and have a few friends dress up to frighten your visitors in the rooms or to jump out at random spots.

Check your insurance policy to make sure you are covered for public liability. And make sure you have a tour guide to ensure that nothing gets stolen from your home.

Advertise your haunted house in school newsletters, along with flyers and a sign out the front of your house.

If you have a group of three people doing this in one house and taking through groups of five visitors at $3 each for a five-minute tour, you could make a few hundred dollars by the end of the night.

140 Shovel snow

It doesn't snow in many parts of Australia, but you just never know. If you live where it snows even occasionally and you have a snow shovel and are quick to clean up, you just might make some money when it does happen to snow.

You will need to door knock when it has snowed to ask if people want you to clear their driveways and paths for a fee. If you live where it really does snow regularly, it would be worth distributing a flyer at the start of the snow season indicating your prices and contact details so you can be contacted when needed.

The rate varies but is usually $10 to $20 a driveway. If it is a very large driveway or area to clear, you can charge more.

141 Make and sell Easter eggs and treats

Unique chocolate Easter eggs can be sold at markets or through friends and family. You could make large ones with a variety of fillings, such as rocky road or Turkish delight, or you could make a variety of small ones — there are lots of options. If you want to turn this into a real business, you could make them for school fundraisers and make more than just Easter eggs, such as various chocolate designs to provide income year-round.

Presentation is very important. Coloured foil, baskets, mini cellophane bags and ribbons can all be used to make them look attractive.

How much you earn depends on the price you sell them for and the cost of ingredients but you could make from $5 an egg.

142 Light up with fireworks

You need a pyrotechnics licence to deal in fireworks and there are lots of rules and regulations that come with this type of work, so it might take a bit of time to get qualified, but it is worth it.

You can do this work outside normal business hours as a second job. Since it is a bit dangerous, there are not a lot of people getting into it. You can easily hurt yourself and you need to really love firecrackers, but it can be very rewarding seeing your designs explode.

You can make thousands of dollars for this work but there is a rather large initial outlay. Most shows charge $2000 to $30000 depending on the size and time of the display, but keep in mind that your costs have to be deducted from these amounts.

143 Freeze and sell ice slabs

This option could only work if you live near a big hill and have a large freezer. You freeze large slabs of ice and then sell them to people who slide down the hill on them. It is heaps of fun and is very popular in summer, especially on hills near beaches.

All you need to do is create the ice blocks, then stick a sign out the front of your house. Drum up more business by letting friends and family know, and by making a flyer and doing a letterbox drop as well as advertising in local shop windows.

You could sell the ice slabs from $10 each. If you have a large freezer, you could make quite a few slabs, generating a few thousand dollars in summer.

144 Work at a polling booth

This is an occasional way to earn money, but since we have to vote, you could spend the day at a polling booth and get paid for it. There are various positions available and even though you won't get a huge amount, you will get paid.

You can work at state and federal elections, and once you have worked at one election you usually get asked to do it again, so you don't necessarily need to reapply.

Take lots of food and water with you as you will be standing all day (most of the positions are standing positions) and you might not get much of a break. The day can be very long, up to 15 hours. It is best to be in good health due to the length of the day and the time you will be on your feet. You need to arrive before voting starts for a quick brief and remain after voting closes to help count votes. For more information, check your local electoral website.

Payment is from $300 depending on your position, although check with your electoral commission for confirmation.

145 Set up an election day stall

On election day you could set up a sausage sizzle near the polling booth entrance and sell drinks, and even handmade crafts. If the voting is located at a school, check that you are allowed to do this first. As an enticement you could offer to donate a percentage of what you make directly to the school.

Food and drink will be popular because people usually have to wait in line and food helps pass the time, especially if they have kids in tow. You could also offer an array of slices and biscuits (check health regulations), and even tea and coffee if it is a cold day.

Most people average in excess of $300 for the day. It takes less time than actually working at the polling booths and depending on how busy you are you may be able to fit in a few more breaks.

146 Work as a fruit picker

Fruit picking doesn't pay a lot, but it can pay for you to travel around the country. Casuals are usually hired for a few months to pick the crops, so it is seasonal work only. However, different fruits and vegetables are ready for picking at different times of the year throughout the country, so you may be able to find work year-round.

All you need to do is locate an orchard and see when it is hiring, or search online for fruit picking work. There are websites available that will show you the crops and when they are ready for picking throughout the year. You need to be fit and fast because you are often paid by the amount you pick instead of per hour.

You are likely to earn around $10 an hour, but free accommodation and meals are often included.

147 Sell sunscreen or drinks at Australia Day events

There are so many events on Australia Day and most people forget to pack sunscreen and regret it severely the next day. Drinks are also often forgotten and everyone needs a drink, especially when it's hot. You could walk around the event (with permission) selling sunscreen or cold drinks.

You could buy the sunscreen in bulk cheaply beforehand then resell it at a higher price, but still within a normal price range. A cooler bag with ice will prevent the sunscreen from getting hot and stop it from going really runny.

If you sell drinks, you will need an esky and a variety of drinks. You won't be allowed to do this at all events as kiosks or food vans will already have been hired, but you won't know unless you ask.

You could make $1 to $2 for a tube of sunscreen and $1 for a can of drink or bottle of water.

148 Sell glow sticks and flashing jewellery on New Year's Eve

If you are heading out to any New Year festivities, why not load yourself up with glow sticks and flashing jewellery to sell to those around you? They are small enough to fill a backpack with plenty and can be bought very cheaply online.

If you get items that don't indicate the year on them, they can be sold at other events, such as parties or the following New Year. An advantage of selling them on New Year's Eve, especially closer to midnight, is that many people are drunk so will buy more!

You can sell them for $1 to $2 each. How much you make will depend on their initial cost, how many you buy and how many you sell.

Part IV

MAKE MONEY
WITH ANIMALS

In this section you will find out how to make money with animals in a variety of fun and interesting ways. From your family pet to livestock, find out how animals can help your money-making ventures.

149 Offer pet minding

Looking after pets in their own home gives peace of mind to the owners while they are away on holiday and allows the pets to feel safe and loved. A typical pet minding visit includes feeding, administering medicines, playing with the animals, cleaning up any messes in the yard or cage and possibly other services as required by the owner.

A visit will take between half an hour to one hour. You can add on services, such as pet grooming, mail collection, taking out and bringing in bins, watering the garden and other things to ensure that the house looks lived in.

You can charge a consultation fee where you will meet the pets, discuss the routine, sign a contract, arrange for a key drop off and pick up fee, a pet transportation fee and more. Make sure you cover everything from the pet's name and how much they eat, to their exercise and what happens if they need to go to the vet. There are also companies that do the entire service and you could be a consultant through them instead of doing this as your own business.

You can charge $20 to $30 per visit, excluding other services that can be added to this fee.

150 Become a dog walker

Many people are too busy to take care of their animals properly and don't have the time to walk their dogs daily. You can get exercise this way, too, and the dogs will get a proper walk.

You can walk one dog at a time or walk them in groups. You can charge more when walking one dog compared with a few dogs at once. If you choose to walk two or more dogs together, do a test walk to see how they interact with each other. You don't want dogs fighting the whole time risking injury to yourself, themselves and any passers-by. You will need to take bags to clean up after the dogs and you will need to give them water, and possibly food (depending on the owner's request), after the walk.

To get started put some flyers up around the neighbourhood and do a letterbox drop. You could also create a website with individual pages stating the services you offer, fees and charges, contact details, customer references or test-imonials and anything else you deem relevant to your business.

You might also consider offering a few people a few hours of free dog walking in exchange for a reference or testimony for your business.

Most dog walkers charge $5 to $15 per half-hour.

 1 5 1 Run a petting zoo

If you have the space and a few animals, you might consider running a petting zoo. You will need an area to house the animals and be able to transport them safely (if you take them to parties and events, otherwise you can set up an enclosure on your property). You'll also need to pay for food, veterinary bills and other specialised care for any of the animals you choose to have, as well as insurance to cover both the animals and public liability.

You can take your zoo to birthday parties, school fairs and schools, or you can set it up at your own house and organise for schools to come to you. Or if you host birthday parties, you can offer two-hour sessions with optional extras such as a birthday cake, party food and lolly bags.

It does cost a bit to set up and initially you won't make much due to expenses. You can earn in excess of $100 an hour after expenses. If you do group bookings, it will be more cost effective.

1 5 2 Pick up dog poo

U18

This is not a glamorous job, but someone has to do it. You could come and pick it up from around your clients' property twice a week and dispose of it for them. They won't even need to be home, so you could do it during school hours, or it's a job that your kids could do. It won't pay big but it's still a money-making option.

You will need gloves, a shovel and a bag to put it in. Some clients may not want you disposing of it in their bin, so you may need to take it home with you and put it in your bin

You can make $5 to $10 a yard depending on the size of the area you cover and how much poo you pick up.

1 5 3 Groom pets

$$

You can groom pets from your home, in a salon or at your client's house. Grooming can involve washing animals, trimming fur and nails, and other services such as worm treatments. If you don't want to start your own business from scratch, there are franchises you can buy into.

You can begin by doing a course if you prefer, but many states don't require it. You will need some experience, as pet grooming does require some skill. You will also need a variety of tools, strength and patience. Many dogs find it scary to be groomed, so you need to be calm as well as strong enough to hold them while you work.

You can charge from $15 for just a bath for a small dog right through to $150 for the works. You can charge even more if you are experienced or have qualifications.

154 Conduct pet funerals

Pet funerals are not a happy pet business but it is a service that is increasing in demand. The initial set-up can be costly, as you will need items such as coffins and memorial stones, and you will have to either create a cemetery on your own land if the council approves or negotiate with a cemetery to use their land.

A pet funeral can be conducted in much the same way as human funerals, with various packages from a basic coffin and a few words right through to silk-lined coffins, headstones and murals.

Contact animal businesses as they will usually be the first to know when someone's pet has died and they can offer a referral. Your business is likely to then grow mostly by word of mouth.

You can charge anything from a few hundred dollars to a few thousand dollars depending on what is required and your expenses.

155 Enter your animal in pet shows

There are many animal shows, pet competitions at showgrounds and events where pets can be exhibited. You can enter your purebred pet or farm animals and, if you win, there are great prizes.

You will need to groom your pet so it is looking its best, ensure it is trained to follow your commands and make sure it is comfortable in front of crowds. You will need to enter your pet well before the event, so check online to see what is happening in your area and any entry requirements.

Prizes vary greatly from $200 right through to thousands of dollars, and even include contracts for TV ads and other modelling jobs.

156 Let your pet become a model or actor

If you live in or near a major city, pet modelling or acting can be quite lucrative if you have the type of animal that agencies are looking for.

For advertisements any animal is appropriate as a huge variety of products use all different types of animals to advertise with, while TV shows often require the more regular kind of pet. It's important that your animal is very well trained so it is best to train it from a young age.

You can contact agencies or search for work yourself online. An agency will organise a portfolio for your pet and will contact you if a suitable part becomes available, so this option is easier than managing it all yourself.

You can make from $200 per advertisement.

 157 Offer horse rides

If you have a well-mannered horse, you could offer horse rides. You could do this at school fairs, parties, horse shows or wherever you keep your horse. Some stables allow you to do horse rides for a fee at their venue. It might not pay a lot but it's a great way to recoup some of the costs of keeping a horse.

Offering horse rides at fairs or private parties is where you will make the most money. Shetland ponies are very popular for this type of work as they are small enough for children to ride easily. Start by offering rides at a few school fairs and ensure you give out business cards to parents.

You could charge $5 to $10 a ride at a fair, or $300 for two hours at a private party.

 158 Offer camel rides

This one might seem a bit out there, but at my school fair and many others I went to as a child you could go on camel rides and it was so much fun.

Camels are not really animals you would keep normally or for a particular use, unlike horses, but they can be good value if you're interested in working with them at events such as fairs and shows. They don't require as much grooming as horses, but they eat and drink a lot. They can also be dangerous, so you need to know how to handle them and do plenty of research before owning one.

Camel rides can be charged from $5 to $10 for quick ones at a fair, or from $150 for long rides along beaches or within parks.

1 5 9   Breed animals

Any animal that you own and have knowledge about you could breed. To maintain a good reputation and the health of your animals, and get the best prices, you must only breed purebred varieties. You must adhere to ethical standards and the regulations set out by animal welfare agencies. You could sell the animals by advertising in the local newspaper, on noticeboards, through pet shops, school newsletters and word of mouth.

You will need a specific, clean area for them to live in. You will also need to care for the babies until they are old enough to be sold. For some animals that is within one week, for others it may not be for a few months. Some animals will require treatment such as microchipping, vaccinations and worming before selling them.

You can sell animals such as chickens for $10 to $20, whereas purebred dogs and cats can fetch over $1000 depending on the breed.

160 Breed and sell heirloom pigs

Heirloom pigs can make money for you in a few ways. Certain breeds of pigs are popular for pets, whereas others are good for meat. Pigs are loyal, intelligent and cleaner than people think, so make excellent pets.

Heirloom pigs are rarer than regular pink pigs. Their meat tends to be fattier but they are tastier as a result. They tend to have a nicer temperament so make better pets. You will need a fair amount of land and somewhere to house them, not to mention providing food and water, but overall they are an easier animal than most to keep.

You can sell them through your local newspaper, at markets or fairs, or talk to your local butcher to see if you can work something out. You could sell a small pet heirloom pig from $50, or from $100 depending on the breed and age of a larger pig. You will get more if it is sold as meat than as a pet.

161 Breed and sell ducks and their eggs

Ducks can make you money by selling their eggs, selling them as meat or by breeding them to sell as they are. Different breeds are suitable for different purposes.

They need room to waddle around as well as somewhere for them to swim a little. They don't need anything as large as a pool or a pond; a container will do as the purpose is more for cleaning than swimming. They love to forage, so they are ideal for controlling pests such as snails but some breeds do like to damage gardens.

Duck eggs tend to be bigger than chicken eggs, and ducks don't lay as many as hens but you can still sell them to family and friends or to your neighbours by putting a sign out the front of your house. You can sell the eggs for $4 to $6 a dozen, or the actual ducks from $20 each.

162 Keep cows

You need a lot of space to keep cows but they are useful for a variety of things, such as for their meat, milk or their calves. Milking cows is a lot of work and the return is often not very good for what is involved. Milking costs a lot to set up and has numerous regulations and machinery requirements.

Keeping cows for meat is an easier option. You need space and to feed them regularly, but they will be pretty happy doing their own thing and then you can either sell them as a whole cow or send them to the abattoir and sell the meat to family and friends.

Fresh, free range and organic meat is increasing in demand, so it is worthwhile getting your farm certified.

You can make upwards of $500 a cow if selling it for meat.

163 Breed sheep

Sheep can be kept for wool or to use the lambs for meat. In case you haven't noticed, lamb is a very expensive meat so breeding sheep would be worth your while.

You will need land for them to roam, food and water, as well as knowing how to care for the lambs when they are born.

You can sell the wool through various websites online, and the meat can be sold at auction or to family and friends. You could also sell the sheepskin separately for slippers and jackets or just as a skin.

You can sell the lambs from $100 each depending on weight. Sheepskins can be sold from $50 for a small skin to over $100 for larger ones. You won't get a lot for wool, probably from only $30 a kilogram.

164 Sell manure

If you have geese, ducks, chickens, horses, sheep, cows or any farm animal really, you can sell their manure.

You can sell it by putting up a sign out the front of your house or try contacting garden shops to see if they will stock it, or even businesses that sell packaged manure and gardening mixes. If a shop is willing to stock it and it sells well, you could contact other farms to see if they are interested in paying you to clean up and dispose of their manure and you could sell this as well.

You will need equipment, such as a shovel, wheelbarrow and trailer, to collect it from your property and to transport it adequately.

You can sell it for $3 a bag from home or probably half that amount to a shop or business.

165 Sell aquariums to businesses

Many businesses like to display an aquarium in their waiting areas or even inside offices as fish have a calming effect. To save them time organising it themselves you could offer a package where you come to the workplace, discuss what they would like, source the materials and fish yourself and then arrange and install it all so they don't have to do a thing.

A good knowledge of fish and setting up aquariums is essential, as well as good sales skills, as this is effectively what you will be doing. Once you have a portfolio showing the different types of fish and aquarium options you offer, start contacting businesses with suitable waiting areas, such as dentists, doctors and companies.

You don't actually need to purchase anything until you get your first order, so it will be relatively cheap to set up. Once you have an order arrange to receive the money or a deposit, then organise what is needed. This way you will never be out of pocket. You can make in excess of $100 per set-up.

166 Service aquariums

Your target market for servicing and cleaning aquariums would be businesses that display them, not so much private homes. You could combine this service with selling the aquarium, as mentioned in the previous entry.

You will need a bit of gear to clean them properly, as well as knowledge about perfect tank conditions, how to fix pumps, and basic fish care to treat any sick fish or ones with simple diseases. To get started simply contact any business you notice that has an aquarium. You could provide this service to private homes if you like but their aquariums are likely to be smaller and will generate less money.

You could offer a weekly or twice-weekly service, depending on your client's needs. You could charge from $50 to clean a large aquarium in an office, depending on how long it takes and what the service includes.

 167 Operate a pet hotel

While this may seem a little out there, many people consider their pets as their children and they want the best level of care for them. Most accommodation doesn't cater for animals, so people have to leave their pets behind when they go on holidays.

Your pet hotel could offer separate areas for each animal, a comfortable bed, home cooked instead of tinned food, an exercise yard and various luxury services. Calming music could be played throughout the hotel.

It would take a bit to set up but you would be able to charge accordingly. For many pampered pooches and felines a pet hotel would make their owners feel much more at ease instead of using a regular kennel service. You could charge in excess of $30 per animal a day.

 168 Become a dog trainer

 Dog training is relatively easy to learn but can be a little difficult with some dog breeds. Once you know what you are doing you could offer private training at people's homes or offer group training lessons at various locations.

Courses are available that can teach you to become a dog trainer. You could do it as a hobby or go right through to qualify as a trainer for guard dogs.

Contact dog groomers, vets, pet shops and breeders to see if they will recommend you or allow you to leave flyers in their place of business.

You can charge from $40 per hour for group lessons or from $60 for private sessions.

1 6 9 Make a dog park

If you have a lot of land, you could fence some off for a dog park. You can choose to charge a fee for dog owners and their dogs to use it, or instead businesses can pay to advertise on its fences. You will probably have more success with the advertising.

You will need to get council approval for the area and it will cost a bit to set it up, but you will make good money from the signs. The area will need to be fully fenced, with jumps and equipment for the dogs to use.

You can advertise through other animal businesses to attract customers as well as offer those businesses a discount on advertising on your fences in exchange for referrals.

You can make in excess of $1000 per sign to appear for a few months depending on the size of the sign, the number of people who use the park and how much exposure the sign gets.

170 Produce a pet training DVD

If you can train animals and are handy with a camera and can edit DVDs, you could create pet training DVDs for people to purchase to train their own pets. Dogs and cats are likely to be the most popular animals, but you could also offer training for other animals such as birds.

You could start with basic commands, such as roll over, sit and beg, and go right through to jumping and show performing.

It could take a little time to get enough good footage, but once your DVD is complete you could try selling it through pet stores, pet groomers and any other animal business, as well as at markets and animal competitions. You could sell the DVDs for $20 to $50 each.

171 Teach fishing

A fishing class can be done on location and can cover all aspects of fishing, such as equipment, how to handle and care for equipment, how to catch fish, common types of fish through to killing, cleaning, storing and cooking or smoking your fish.

A fully comprehensive class will take from one to two days. You could arrange them through a community college or contact local hotels, campgrounds and tour groups to work out a package deal. Local high schools might even be interested in you teaching their students.

It will cost a bit to set up if you provide everything such as rods and tackle, or you can request that your students bring these items with them and you provide everything else. You could charge from $100 a day for a class.

172 Teach fly fishing

You could also teach people how to do fly fishing. You can supply all of the necessary equipment or provide a list of required tools that your students must bring with them on the day, such as fishing rod, waders and tackle. You then get everyone to meet at a certain location and show them how to do it.

You could advertise your group classes in newspapers or through tackle shops, campgrounds, tour groups and community colleges. You will need to check local council rules since teaching a class in a river may require a permit.

You could charge from $80 per person per class, more if you are providing the equipment.

173 Operate fishing charters

A fishing charter will be expensive to set up because you will need a boat, fishing rods and lifejackets as well as adequate insurance, but if you love to fish and already own a boat, it won't cost too much.

Before you begin you will need to decide the hours you will operate, as well as policies about whether sessions will run if the weather is too dangerous to go out and if will you offer full or partial refunds if a session needs to be cancelled.

You can advertise through tackle shops, information and tourist centres, local shops such as takeaway outlets, or try and connect with national caravan parks, tour companies and other travel businesses to cross-promote or become part of a package deal.

You can charge from $100 depending on the length of each trip and what is included.

 174 Teach a 'how to cook your catch' class

A 'how to cook your catch' class would be a great community college or on-location class about cooking seafood. You can choose to fish first for a few hours and then teach people how to clean and cook what they have caught, or just teach the cooking side of things.

If you are only focussing on the cooking aspect, you can teach the lesson at a community college kitchen and select which seafood dishes you will cook, such as smoked salmon, beer-battered flathead or garlic prawns. If you do it on location, you will need to know beforehand which fish is likely to be caught and have the appropriate ingredients on hand to make something with what they catch.

If you arrange to teach at a community college, you will automatically be promoted through its advertising. Doing it yourself can be harder but you can advertise with local businesses.

You can charge from $100 per person depending on such things as how many classes you teach, how many dishes are taught, the cost of ingredients and the location of the class.

Part V

MAKE MONEY WITH CARS

Cars are very expensive items to own. There are ways you can reduce the cost of ownership or generate a wage by using your car. The ideas in this section are based on using your own car to make money or making money from other cars.

175   Drive the car pool

When you car pool, instead of alternating who drives, why not offer to drive every time? Those you car pool with will chip in for your petrol and you do the driving. Since you are all going to the same place, it will usually be cheaper for them to give you petrol money rather than drive themselves. It will also save wear and tear on their cars and is more environmentally friendly.

Send an email out to your work colleagues to find out who might be interested. In the email state where you live, where you would be willing to pick people up from, what time you start and finish work, and how much you would like for petrol.

Depending on how far you travel, the going rate is usually $20 to $30 a week but it is up to you to reach an agreement with your colleagues.

176   Become a taxi driver

To work as a taxi driver you can go with a company and work when it suits you, or be a specialised weekend taxi for family and friends so when they are too drunk to drive they pay you to drive them home.

It is a hard occupation with a lot of risks involved. More often than not you will deal with drunken people and not only can they be rude and obnoxious, they can vomit in your car, threaten you and do runners instead of paying the proper fare.

The shifts are usually 12 hours long, but if you are just doing it for family and friends on weekends you needn't work those hours. You will need a car that is registered specifically as a taxi if you are doing it for more than family and friends.

You can make around $300 a shift. The good money is made during the evening, but you can still make money during the day.

177 Become a chauffeur

There are many companies that require chauffeurs and if you have a good driving record, you will more than likely be considered. You may offer your service for just one person whenever they require it, or you could work set hours with a company, making it more possible to pick and choose the hours that you work.

The work doesn't involve as many risks as taxi driving because you are usually dealing with businesspeople. It can be a fairly tedious job but it does offer various shifts. You will need to be well groomed and speak clearly.

You can usually make in excess of $200 a day.

178 Provide car detailing

If you enjoy cleaning cars, step it up and detail them properly, with waxing and the complete works. You will need equipment such as a good vacuum cleaner with attachments, an upholstery cleaner, polish, buffers, a bucket, car and wheel cleaner, polishing pads, a toothbrush for cleaning small spaces and a microfibre cleaning cloth.

It takes time to perfect car detailing, especially as different cars require different treatment. It can take a few hours to do each job properly but you can charge accordingly. Getting started is simply a matter of putting the word out with flyers, emails and word-of-mouth recommendations.

Start off by offering free detailing to build your reputation and receive testimonials. Set up a website to post pictures of your work, your list of services, prices, contact details and your testimonials.

You can provide your service to car dealerships, real estate agents (they need their cars to look good) and businesspeople. You could do it privately at people's homes or from office building car parks. You can charge from $200 a detail.

1 7 9 Offer car towing

To do this work you can either invest in a car trailer or towing equipment or have an actual tow truck. If you chose to do it for a bit of cash on the side, when you see an accident you can pull up and offer to tow for a fee. Tow companies charge a few hundred dollars for this service, so if you won't be travelling far you could charge $100. People without car insurance will be very interested, and depending on where you live you might find most people are uninsured and won't be getting a $250 refund for the towing through their insurance, making your price very appealing.

Get some business cards and hand them out to friends and family. Make sure you have them on you at all times, so if you ever see an accident, you can offer your service. Also put signage on your trailer so when others see you towing they can keep you in mind.

Check your current insurance policy to ensure you are covered when towing cars. Use a receipt book and offer customers a receipt, which they need to sign and say they have paid you as well as confirm that they have received their car. You can easily make from $100 for a short tow.

1 80 Provide an airport shuttle service

If you live reasonably close to the airport, providing a shuttle service to and from the airport could be a popular idea. If you have a van, you could offer your service for groups, or if you have a car, offer it to businesspeople. You could also contact a few hotels and work out an arrangement with them.

You want to aim to provide a more personal service than a taxi or chauffer service. Ideally your car will be modern, but it must be immaculately kept, and you need to drive well and be reliable. You will need a back-up plan in case anything goes wrong with your car.

You could distribute flyers informing people of your service and the prices you charge. Also make business cards and hand them out to family and friends. Regular business might take a while to develop, but if you live close to an airport, you should be quite busy.

You can charge from $40 per person per trip, depending on the distance travelled.

181 Organise body delivery

When people die, someone needs to move the body from A to B. That someone could be you and you could charge a fair bit for this service as it's not a job most people want to do. I know someone who started doing this on the side and ended up so busy and making so much money that they quit their job. Now with some family members they do this full time, earning more than ever before.

To do this you need a car with a space big enough to transport a body. If you are going to be covering some distance, it is better if the car is refrigerated. You will probably want to use a separate car other than your main means of transport due to the odour associated with death. In this car you will need a gurney to move the body and you will also need to employ someone to assist you.

You will need to wear protective gear such as overalls, gloves and a mask. You will more than likely come into contact with bodily fluids, so you want to be fully clothed and protected.

You can charge upwards of $150 for this service.

182 Deliver flowers

Some florists have delivery services, some do it themselves. If you would like to deliver flowers, find out the going delivery rate in your area then contact the local florists with a proposal.

You will usually need to do a run early in the morning, then a few more during the day. Start with one florist, as you can always work for more if you have the time. You will need a van that has air-conditioning to ensure the flowers you are transporting remain fresh.

The really busy days such as Valentine's Day and Mother's Day will have you run off your feet. If you are only interested in doing this casually, these are days to work. You could also give your details to the florists in your area and they can contact you on their really busy days if they need extra deliveries made.

How much you make will vary greatly depending on whether you charge hourly or per delivery and the distance of the deliveries, but you can expect to make from $150 for a four-hour shift if your work for yourself, less if you are employed by a florist.

1 8 3 Offer wedding and formals car hire

If you have a nice car, you could rent it out for weddings and formals. You will need to keep your car in immaculate condition, ensuring that it is detailed regularly so it's always presentable. You will need more than your basic car insurance because you will be driving a variety of strangers around; it would also be wise to have public liability insurance.

You need to work out how much you will charge, whether hourly, per day or per evening. Will you add a surcharge if you are asked to drive to a few places en route rather than just to and from an event?

There are certain times of the year that will be busier than others—September to December is heavy wedding and formal season, and from November to December you'll have the Christmas period with people attending lots of parties and various events. You will more than likely have more work during these few months than throughout the rest of the year.

You can charge in excess of $200 depending on your type of car and the length of hire.

184 Offer backpacker car hire

If you have a few older cars that are reliable, such as vans, you could hire them to backpackers who want to see the country. Backpackers don't normally want to spend a fortune on car hire and many don't want to buy cars either. Older-model vans are especially popular as backpackers often travel together in groups.

In fact, there are a few companies already doing this as it is beneficial for all involved. You simply buy some cheap older vans in good mechanical condition and hire them out and you would make your money back fairly quickly.

You need to work out the rates you will charge, including additional fees such as insurance and administration fees, which you would add to the rate, how long the vehicles can be hired for, the number of kilometres that can be driven before being charged for extra kilometres and so on.

There will be a bit of outlay initially, but once word gets around and you get some good reviews it will more than pay for itself. Expect to charge $30 per car per day.

185 Run a backpacker car yard

Older cars could be bought and sold from a backpacker car yard. These would ideally be located in capital cities near airports as this is where backpackers arrive and depart.

You could have vehicles ranging in price from $500 to $5000. You can choose to operate every day at a particular location or do a once-weekly auction at a location hired for the occasion.

You could set up a website and place it on travel forums. You could also advertise with the main travel agencies, which may be expensive at first but it's also probably where you will get the majority of your business.

You could offer backpackers a buyback service at the end of their trip so they don't need to worry about selling the car, allowing you to resell it a few times over, generating more profit. You can make from $200 per car.

186 Offer long–distance car delivery

If you travel frequently, you could offer a long-distance car delivery service. Say someone bought a car online that is miles away from where they live but you happen to be near where it's located, you could drive the car to them for a fee. If you have already travelled to that area for work, you could pocket the travel allowance you were given and make extra money by returning home in someone's new car.

Many people buy cars all over the country now as the best prices can be found outside capital cities. And not everyone has the time to travel to their new car's location to drive it home. You could offer to do it for them. You would need to work out the hourly rate you would charge for driving their car, including petrol and insurance costs.

Depending on how far you have to drive, you could make from $100 per trip.

187 Provide a party bus

If you have a bus, you could convert it to a party bus for people to hire to get from place to place. Deck it out with seats, a dance floor and a juke box, and make the interior look like a nightclub. This would be especially popular for hens' and bucks' nights. You could offer different packages, such as from a restaurant to a club, or a full hens' or buck's party, which would include a few hours on the bus rather than just an hour to get from here to there.

Making the service for a minimum amount of guests per booking ensures it will be worth your time. For smaller groups you could charge a set fee instead of per head.

Set clear rules about alcohol, such as how much can be consumed and possible breath tests to ensure the safety of all involved. While alcohol can't be consumed on your bus without a licence, your guests will still be drinking elsewhere.

You will also need adequate insurance in case anyone hurts themselves on the bus or you are involved in an accident.

A party bus is typically hired for $200 for one hour to get from a restaurant to a club. You could make in excess of $500 for hens' or bucks' parties for just a few hours' work.

188 Hire out your car

Hiring out your car while you are away is one way to make a little cash. If you are renting your house out, you could also offer your car for an extra fee. Another alternative if you have a second car that you don't use on weekends is to rent it to people to use for a low fee.

You will need to ensure your insurance covers other people driving your car. Your most likely customers will be your friends and family, who can then spread the word to their friends and family. You could make from $20 a day for renting out your car.

189 Become a driving instructor

For this work you can either be employed by a driving school or run your own business by converting your car. Now that people are required to complete more driving hours than ever before they get their driver's licence, the demand for driving instructors is huge.

It will cost you a bit to add the controls to the passenger side of your car but you will be able to recoup your costs fairly quickly. Not everyone does the conversion, but it makes driving safer and keeps insurance costs down.

Once you are set up you can advertise with secondary schools and colleges and offer a special discount for students or a discount when more than one family member uses your services. You can charge from $50 per hour for a private lesson.

190 Deliver pizzas

Pizza and takeaway outlets are always looking for drivers. Look for signs in their windows advertising a job and all you need to do is apply. The hours are not conducive for a great social life as your shifts will most often be evenings and weekends, but it can be a good way to make money, with no qualifications other than a valid driver's licence required.

Some places do allow you to use their cars, but if not some signage may be put on your car during your shift.

You can make from $12 an hour plus $2 per delivery depending on the times and days you work.

191 Deliver nappies

Some people like to use cloth nappies as they are more environmentally friendly, but don't want to wash them. Nappy delivery services pick up and drop off nappies and all you need do is drive the truck. You just need a valid driver's licence.

The working hours are often during school time, making this a good job for any parent. Check the *Yellow Pages* for companies that deliver nappies in your area and contact them to find out if they need drivers. You can also check the employment classifieds in newspapers or on employment websites. For this work you can make about $20 to $30 per hour.

192 Become a courier

You can become a courier either by starting your own business or by working for an established company. Some companies will give you a vehicle to drive, while others prefer you to use your own.

All you need is a valid driver's licence and you will be trained according to their delivery system. You will need to be an early riser as you will often have 6 am starts. A good knowledge of your city is useful, but not essential as you can use a GPS.

These jobs are usually advertised in the employment classifieds in newspapers and online. Otherwise contact the company you would like to work for directly. You can make from $20 an hour.

193 Become a long-distance courier

Courier work is also required between cities. If you already travel a bit, you could offer a courier service when you are on the road. You could do this predominately for friends and family, unless you want to set up a proper courier service for interstate work.

Essentially you could deliver or pick up packages wherever you are going for a fee. If you have enough deliveries, this would more than cover your travel expenses.

To get started, let your friends and family know you are offering this service and it will spread by word of mouth. If you plan to set up a proper full-time business, you will need to advertise accordingly. You can make in excess of $100 a trip.

194 Work as a truck driver

Being a truck driver can be quite hard work unloading deliveries, travelling interstate and driving for long hours, but you can make good money.

To drive big trucks you need a specific truck licence. Once you have one, either check newspaper job classifieds or contact companies directly. You will often see signs out the front of businesses stating 'Drivers Wanted'.

You will frequently be away for most of the week or on weekends doing back-to-back deliveries, so it can be hard for families, but it is something anyone can do once you get a truck licence.

Your base rate is likely to be $18 to $25 per hour, but you will be paid overtime and other bonuses making your wage much higher.

195   Provide a removalist service

A removalist service can be done on a large interstate scale or you could do a smaller intercity service. If you are starting with just yourself and one employee and one truck, an intercity service is easier.

You will need a truck, a trolley to move large items, packaging materials and access to cheap boxes you can sell or rent to customers. It will also be easier if you employ another person to help you while you're getting started. This might suit you for the long term as there are quite a few removalists who are small operations. You will also need good insurance in case anything goes wrong during the move.

How much you charge will vary widely depending on the size of the goods you are moving and how far you are moving them. You could make from $500 for a small move.

Part VI

MAKE MONEY WITH

DOMESTIC IDEAS

Making money from cleaning or personal services is a great option if you have no qualifications or need a way to make money while you are at home looking after children. Many of these ideas can be done outside business hours and are relatively easy to set up.

196 Become a domestic personal shopper

There are a few ways you can offer domestic personal shopping, such as assisting the elderly by picking up their medicines and personal items, or by purchasing groceries and anything else required for others. Doing people's shopping, as long as they are specific about what they want, can be a great way to earn money.

Put an ad in your local newspaper or distribute flyers to get the word out. Retirement villages or Over 55 complexes are great places to start. This will appeal to many older people who don't want to shop online.

You can earn $10 to $20 an hour depending on what is required.

197 Offer house cleaning for mums with newborns

A mother who has just given birth would welcome someone to clean her home. You could organise a three-month contract to do a clean and tidy twice weekly, including cleaning the bathroom or kitchen or even just a mop and sweep.

You just need some good cleaning products to get started, and it is something that can be done around school hours, so it's great for those with children of their own.

You can market your service as a great baby shower gift for friends to give the mum to be. It is up to you if you charge per hour or per job. Some charge from $25 an hour; others charge from $50 to include oven cleaning, $80 to clean a bathroom and so on.

198 Become a mummy's helper

You can become a mummy's helper by assisting new mothers after birth. Many women don't live near their mothers and need some reassurance and help when they first arrive home from hospital. For some new mums even simple things such as changing nappies or bathing a baby can be daunting.

You could offer a service where you show new mums various aspects of looking after their newborn, as well as look after their baby for a few hours so mum can sleep. To give advice on breastfeeding matters you need to be a qualified lactation consultant, so unless you have this qualification you could not include breastfeeding assistance with your services.

A common rate for this work is from $20 an hour.

199 Offer babysitting

Babysitting can be a relatively easy way to earn money. The hours are flexible and sometimes it can be a matter of getting paid to watch TV. The rate of pay is up to you but there are a few factors that can vary your price, such as age, experience, qualifications, the amount of time you will be working (for example, overnight) and how many children you will be minding. It is advisable to have first-aid certification to ensure everyone's safety, although not everyone expects it (especially not from teenagers).

Make sure the payment and what is involved is very clear, such as details on how to get to their house, the number of hours you will be required, will the children have already eaten or will you be cooking for them and if the children have particular night-time rituals or special needs.

The going rate is usually $10 to $20 an hour, with more charged for very late nights and if you are minding extra children, while sleepovers start from around $120 for the night.

200 Organise garage sales

Many people like the idea of having a garage sale but don't want the hassle of organising everything. You could offer a service where you do everything necessary to get organised, such as pricing, advertising and setting up, then all they need to do is be there for the sale. Alternatively you could offer to host it as well, but it could end up costing them more than it is worth.

Depending on where you live and the services you include, you could charge either from $15 an hour or a percentage of the money made at the sale.

201 Wash windows

There is a surprising amount of work around for window washers. All businesses use them, even those in large shopping centres. You need very little equipment and no experience, although referrals are handy.

You can pretty much select your hours and rate of pay; then it is simply a matter of finding shops or homes who want your service. Most shops will want you to wash their windows weekly or possibly twice weekly, whereas private homes will need you to come less often.

You can charge around $5 per pane of glass (1 metre × 1 metre), while large windows and commercial jobs will cost more. You could charge $150 to $200 for an average home.

202 Clean swimming pools

Most people don't have time to clean their swimming pool themselves but it needs to be done regularly. You will need some equipment to do a proper job, such as a net to scoop out leaves as well as a kit to test the chlorine levels to ensure they are correct and safe for swimming.

Offer a discount for the homes you do regularly as an incentive to keep you coming back. Regular cleaning means the job is smaller each time instead of doing irregular large jobs, which will take longer but you can charge more for.

Most pool cleaners start their prices at $50, but each fee you charge will depend on what is involved.

203 Offer house sitting

You can get paid for house sitting, while others will do it for free. All you really need to do is stay at someone's house while they are away. You collect the mail, keep the house clean, maintain it and make it looked lived in, so it's less likely to be broken into. This is a great way to save on paying rent as sometimes you can get house sitting jobs for three months or longer.

To find a house to mind there are websites you can subscribe to, or you can let people know you're interested. You can get a surprising amount of work just by word of mouth. Whenever you finish house sitting jobs, ask for a reference, which you can show to future house sitting clients. This will make them more comfortable than leaving their home with a stranger.

How much you make depends on the price you agree on, but you can easily get in excess of $50 a week.

204   Offer house minding

Instead of house sitting where you are actually living in the home you could mind houses. When people are away you go to the house, check on it, collect mail, tidy and water the garden, and generally make it look lived in.

Not everyone likes the idea of having someone living in their home but they do want someone to keep an eye on it while they are away. The bonus for you is that you could actually do a few houses at once instead of just house sitting one.

To get started post some flyers on community noticeboards, do a letterbox drop and contact local travel agents, which might be willing to refer you or at least display your flyers in their office. Smaller travel agents are more likely to do this than the big chains.

Depending on how long you are looking after a house, exactly what is required and how many houses you are doing, you could easily make $50 or more a week.

 ## 205 Start a natural cleaning company

More and more people are turning to natural alternatives to clean their homes. Instead of using harsh chemicals you could clean using natural ingredients. There is lots of information online about cleaning with simple products such as bicarbonate of soda and vinegar instead of bleach and other chemicals. This will appeal especially to those with allergies and those who prefer to be environmentally friendly. It is cheaper to clean with natural products as well.

Sometimes cleaning with natural products can take a bit longer than when using harsh chemicals, but your clients will be able to come home to a lovely fresh house without being overpowered by the smell of bleach in their bathrooms, and you will also benefit from not having to use harmful products. You could make upwards of $25 per hour.

 ## 206 Teach natural cleaning methods

Instead of cleaning people's homes you could teach them how to clean their houses in an environmentally friendly way using products they probably already own.

You could do a one- to two-hour session in people's homes showing them how to clean the bathroom and oven, remove clothing stains, and wash windows and floors, all with natural products. You could provide a booklet for them to outline which products to use and where, for example floors or windows.

You won't need to do much cleaning yourself—instead you are simply showing them how to do it and then they can do it themselves. You could make around $100 a session.

207 Get rid of cobwebs

This might sound silly, but so many people are afraid of spiders and don't want to clear their own cobwebs. Pest control only sprays the area but you are still left with the cobwebs. If pest control has been done properly, it should keep webbing spiders away for 12 months, so you may only need to do it annually.

All you would need to do is remove cobwebs with a broom, either by standing on a ladder or using a long-handled broom. It is then a good idea to wipe the area with lemon oil as it deters spiders. You could use a separate mop or cloth for this, or apply the oil to a towel that is clipped to the end of your broom.

To get started, offer your service to a few friends or family and get them to refer you. Also create a flyer and do a letter box drop. Depending on the size of the house and how much work is involved you could charge from $50 per home.

208 Clean offices

While cleaning an office is essentially the same as cleaning a house, it is usually done daily after business hours. It is a great job for anyone with children and a partner at home in the evenings. Your main duties would involve vacuuming, emptying bins, cleaning toilets, replacing toilet paper, tidying kitchenettes and so on. The size of the office space will determine how long it takes you.

Some offices will have a custodial cupboard containing all of your equipment and supplies, while others will require you to provide these items. You can charge more if you have to supply all your own equipment and cleaning supplies.

Check the offices in your area to see if they are looking for a cleaner or if they know of any businesses that may require your services; some businesses contract cleaners through cleaning companies while others hire privately. You could also check banks to see if they can use your services. You could charge upwards of $25 per hour.

209 Clean trucks

Cleaning trucks can pay really well as it is not something many people do. It is a big job, but if you have the right equipment and some good contracts, you can make some decent cash. Getting started and establishing a good reputation is probably the hardest part, but once you are set up and people know who you are and start recommending you to their friends, you will have plenty of work.

To begin contact smaller delivery businesses and go from there. You will need a reputation and experience before you can get contracts with large national companies.

Then call or approach businesses that use trucks, present them with your offer and maybe a discount valid for the next two to four weeks to get business. You could also offer a bonus or an extra service if they refer you to other businesses who also take up your offer.

You can make from $100 a truck depending on the size of the truck and the amount of work required.

210 Clean house cladding

Due to water restrictions many people can't hose down their homes, and homes with cladding can begin to look rather dirty. Once cleaned, the results are amazing and highly recommended for those looking at selling. To do this work you will need to get a pressure cleaner and water exemption.

To get started contact real estate agents and ask if they will recommend you to their clients when they are selling to make the houses look better and sell for a higher price. Also contact anyone who has anything to do with renovations or repairs to see if they are interested in cross-promotion (where you recommend them and they recommend you).

You can charge $100 to $500 for an average home, another $100 to $500 to do a driveway, and more for roofs and gutters. For a price breakdown the rate per square metre is around $1 to $2.

211 Clean and paint roofs

You need high-pressure equipment to clean a roof properly, but they will look great afterwards. Cleaning your roof is recommended if you are selling your home or if you have painted or rendered the exterior, because a dirty old roof will age the whole house. While you are cleaning the roof you could also offer a repainting service to finish the look.

The easiest way to get yourself out there is to contact real estate agents to ask if they will recommend you to their clients, or to contact other tradespeople and ask if they are interested in cross-promotion. You can charge from $100 just for cleaning or upwards of $500 for painting.

 2 1 2 Clean churches

Cleaning churches isn't quite the same as regular cleaning as churches contain many old items that need special care, not to mention intricately carved pieces that can take some time to clean and items that will require polishing. Consequently, cleaning a church properly will take a lot longer than a private home.

You could market yourself directly to churches, or even consider marketing your service through bridal magazines, bridal events and bridal stores for post-wedding cleaning. It will be one less thing for brides or family to think about or to have to do on or after the big day.

You could charge $100 or higher depending on what is involved and the size of the church.

 2 1 3 Work as a pest controller

Pests such as cockroaches, spiders and other insects and rodents are a problem in many homes, especially in summer.

It can take a bit of cash to get set up but once you are organised, you can make a lot of money.

Ask real estate agents if they will refer you to landlords because many houses need a treatment between tenants. As an enticement, offer a special real estate price.

Do a flyer drop and make sure you have signage on your car as you will be noticed when driving around between jobs.

For a treatment inside and out you can charge from $250 or more to treat German cockroaches.

214 Clean before open home inspections or before and after rental agreements

When people are trying to sell their home they usually keep it as clean as possible, but if it gets a full-service clean before open home inspections it is much more likely to sell. Rental properties also often need to be cleaned properly once tenants have moved out or before new ones move in. And renters often use professional cleaners at the end of a lease to avoid disputes about the cleanliness of the property and make it easier to get their bond refunded.

Contact real estate agencies to ask if they will refer you to their clients. You could offer a real estate discount or give them a percentage of the bill as an incentive. Specialising in real estate cleaning is an excellent way to ensure ongoing work.

You could charge upwards of $200 depending on what is required.

215 Clean schools

Kids sure know how to make a mess and they do this really well at school. Primary and secondary schools need to be cleaned daily, including everything from vacuuming to the toilets.

Some schools have their own cleaning supplies, so you needn't buy your own; these jobs will simply be a matter of sorting out your hours and how much you will be paid. At other schools you will need to supply your own equipment and supplies, so will need to buy items such as a backpack vacuum cleaner (otherwise you will create back and postural problems), cleaning sprays and cloths. As schools are usually quite large they will also often require a full clean every school holidays.

You can charge $50 and upwards per hour but check the rates charged at other schools in your area for price comparisons.

216 Clean out garages

No-one likes to clean out their garage and I am truly shocked at how many people sell their home and leave their garage full of junk for the new owner to deal with. Other people just store everything in the garage and it ends up piling up and up.

Your service could come and clear out a garage without the owner needing to think about it. You would simply load everything required in a trailer truck or a skip and remove it, as well as sweep out the garage for them.

Another option you could offer is to assist an owner to clean their garage with them. You go to their home for a specified time and sort through the garage with them. Anything they don't want can be removed by you instantly. It is usually easy to get rid of junk if you're with someone who has no attachment to any of it, which is where you would come in.

To get started you can contact real estate agencies and tradespeople to recommend you, or distribute flyers advertising your service. You could make from $25 an hour.

2 1 7   Paint numbers on wheelie bins

Wheelie bins or rubbish bins sometimes get stolen or damaged. They are much easier to identify if they have a house number painted on them.

Painting numbers on wheelie bins is a rather simple job that you can make more unique by offering different styles, or include names instead of numbers, for example 'Jones 25 Fair Ave'.

You could do a flyer drop or do a doorknock around your neighbourhood to get started. Also contact your local council or waste management facility to ask if they will recommend your services because it will save everyone money by being able to identify and return bins.

You could charge per number or letter, or just a flat rate of $5 to $10 per bin.

2 1 8   Clean wheelie bins

This can be a particularly disgusting job. The inside of wheelie bins can get very dirty and stinky, but this job can be done relatively quickly and easily by using a pressure cleaner. This service is particularly needed over summer when green waste in bins composts very quickly and attracts pests.

You could promote yourself through your local council and waste management facility or by distributing flyers. When cleaning you could add a spray to deter bugs to ensure the bins stay cleaner for longer. A clean bin is going to mean fewer pests around, so your service will be beneficial to all.

You could charge $10 a bin depending on what you do and the state of the bin.

2 1 9   Clean carpets

You will need to outlay some money to buy the right equipment, but many people who have gone into carpet cleaning have found it very lucrative.

Once you are organised, contact schools (in particular private schools), businesses and real estate agencies to offer your services. If your work is good, real estate agencies are likely to use your services regularly for cleaning rentals, while schools will most likely need you during school holidays, banks and larger businesses a few times a year and private businesses once yearly.

You can make upwards of $200 for a basic house or from $2000 for a school. I know of someone who left a highly paid government job and is now making more money cleaning carpets!

220 Remove graffiti

Graffiti is everywhere, and it's not often that people and businesses like to keep it on their fences, signs and property. This is where you come in. Removing graffiti is not an easy job but with the right equipment and chemicals it can be done. When getting set up ensure you have a logo on both your uniform and your vehicle as people will notice you while you are removing graffiti and are likely to call you for work.

Contact schools as they regularly get graffitied. To get started you could offer to do one free removal in exchange for an ad in the school newsletter. Distribute flyers as well, especially in graffiti-prone areas and to the businesses you can see that have been graffitied.

Most graffiti removal companies charge $100 to $200 per square metre for the first one to two metres and about a third of that price for subsequent metres.

221 Clean curtains and blinds

Curtains and blinds often get overlooked in a home but they can get extremely dirty. Hiring a professional is the best way to clean them, especially at the end of a lease.

You will need a van with all of your equipment in the back to enable ease of cleaning. To get started contact restaurants as well as private homes. Restaurants are more likely to get their blinds and curtains cleaned regularly due to health regulations. This will often be every second month, so it would be good regular work in comparison to once a year or less for most homes.

You can charge $10 or so per small blind, much more for larger blinds, and often around $200 or more for a regular home with a few small blinds and a few large blinds.

222 Clean up building sites

Building sites get into a terrible mess and need to be tidied. A builder can do it, but will charge an arm and a leg for it as it is not worth their time. This work isn't restricted to just actual building sites either but anywhere that has been renovated or had tradespeople coming through.

Building sites are usually littered with wood offcuts, wire pieces and all manner of discarded items, not to mention the rubble and dirt. Cleaning them is often quite a large job and very physically demanding. Sites where tradespeople have been doing repairs or renovations are not usually as bad.

To advertise your business contact tradespeople to see if they will recommend you to their clients or book you to clean up after them. Contact property developers, too, as they will have ongoing work. For this work you can make $25 to $50 an hour.

223 Provide personal care

People who are sick or injured need looking after. If they are unable to do it themselves, they need to be bathed, helped to get dressed, fed and so on. You could choose to be employed by an agency or do it yourself.

Some agencies will require qualifications, some will help you arrange qualifications and train you, and others just need you to do the basics so no qualifications will be necessary. If you decide to work on your own, contact hospitals and doctors to ask if they will recommend you or display your flyer in their office.

The work you do will depend on your level of experience and qualifications but it usually involves shopping, bathing, dressing and general personal maintenance. You can make $20 to $30 an hour.

224 Become an aged-care worker

The population is ageing and there is a never-ending need for aged-care workers. Many older people prefer not to leave their homes to live in aged-care homes, making in-home aged-care very popular. You could go around daily to check on the elderly, clean and tidy for them, provide meals and other support services.

Otherwise you could work in an aged-care home. Many aged-care homes will employ you and then train you to get the necessary qualifications. As your qualifications increase, so will your work responsibilities and your wage.

It can be a very demanding job physically, so you need to be fit. It can also be emotionally draining at times but those who do it usually find it very rewarding work. You can make upwards of $20 an hour.

225   Clean up after people have died

This is a job you need a very strong stomach for and most can't do it. When someone dies the body is removed, but the mess is left behind. It is not a job most people want to think about but it is necessary.

To do this type of work you will need to check if there are any regulations in your area and how to dispose of biohazards. It is not an easy business to set up as a lot of necessary protective gear and equipment is required, as well as permits, but it is something you would make a lot of money from.

When you are ready contact police stations, funeral homes and anywhere that deals with death to see if you can secure some work or if they will recommend you.

You can charge around $600 an hour due to the high costs involved in running this sort of business and the fact that no-one wants to do it.

226   Become a household organiser

Many people live in absolute chaos and could do with someone teaching them how to organise their home.

Being a household organiser is similar to working as a life coach, but instead you visit your client's homes and help them to declutter by sorting through their papers and personal effects, create a budget using systems they can work with and organise realistic schedules so their domestic lives can run more efficiently. You could also add cleaning to your service.

You could charge from $20 an hour for your organising services.

227 Teach a 'just moved out of home' class

Not everyone knows how to cook, clean and take care of themselves properly when they first move out of home. Many people don't have a clue about budgeting or handling money efficiently.

For those who have just moved out of home and fall in this category you could run a class that teaches general domestic skills such as basic cooking, how to create a budget and pay bills, how to clean quickly and effectively, and how to wash and iron.

You could offer gift certificates so parents and relatives could give the lessons as a house warming present. Also contact local colleges and universities to ask if you can advertise on campus or if you could run workshops there. Also contact older groups as there are many divorcees who could use a class like this, too.

You could charge from $120 for 10 classes that cover everything—ideally run through a community college as evening classes. If you have 10 students per two-hour class and run three classes a week, you could make $3600 over the 10-week period for a couple of hours of your time a week.

228 Clean stables

Cleaning stables is a labour-intensive job, but it needs to be done. This work could be done at stables or at private homes.

You will have to remove all the muck in the stables, clean them out, and replace straw as well as possibly feed. It may take a while to complete but the more you do it the quicker you will get.

If you are working for yourself, you may need to buy gumboots, gloves, a shovel and other equipment. Many stables will have most of what you need, so it shouldn't be too expensive to start up. You can earn from $20 an hour.

229 Mow lawns

While there are many lawnmowing businesses out there already, more and more people want their lawns mown and businesses actually have to turn down work.

You could buy into a franchise or you can do it yourself. You will need a good lawnmower, a trimmer and a vehicle large enough to transport them. Then it is simply a matter of putting out flyers and getting work.

Once you have a few customers you will find that most people want to book you for every two to three weeks, so you will have continual work. You can charge $50 for a small lawn and over $100 for a large lawn.

230 Become a gardener

Not everyone has time for their garden and if it is unattended for too long it can quickly become a jungle of weeds. A well-landscaped garden adds value to a home, sometimes as much as $10 000.

You can offer a variety of services from weeding and mowing lawns to trimming hedges, watering and planting. You need some knowledge about plants to be a good gardener. You will also need some tools, such as gloves, a shovel and fork, edge trimmer, lawnmower and a wheelbarrow.

Your best advertisements will be the gardens you maintain, but to get continual work you will need to deliver flyers around your neighbourhood and keep your own garden looking beautiful. You can make from $30 an hour by gardening.

231 Clean out gutters

Roof gutters get clogged with leaves, which can become a very expensive hazard. You don't want to have dried leaves in gutters during bushfire season because embers can start roof fires, and in winter they can clog up causing roof flooding. You can clean them easily with a ladder, gloves, bucket and trowel.

To get clients you could walk around your neighbourhood looking at gutters and offer your services door to door; or offer a special discount if they use your services that day or week. Provided you are not scared of heights, this can be a simple way to make some money.

You could charge per hour or depending on the house size, such as $20 an hour or $50 per house.

232 Teach beekeeping

Lots of people want to keep bees but don't know where to start. If you already keep bees, you could teach your customers this skill before selling them the bees, or offer general classes on beekeeping from your home or local community college. You could teach everything from the equipment to use right through to breeding and selling bees. You could provide all of the equipment or provide a list of items for your students to bring when attending your course.

Advertise through newspapers and community noticeboards, or start by offering your course in community colleges. When you are established you should be able to rely on word of mouth.

You could charge from $150 a course, with a higher fee if you provide all the equipment.

233 Grow and make herb bunches

Herbs are very easy to grow from seed and grow quite quickly. If you grow your own herbs, you could sell bunches of them at local markets. They could be sold fresh or dried, and you could create your own dried herb mixes such as Italian herbs.

You don't need a huge garden to grow herbs. They can grow in anything, even leftover margarine containers on your window sill, so you can grow a few varieties in a small space.

Besides markets you could approach local businesses, such as small supermarkets, delis or cafes, to see if they would be interested in buying from you. Since homegrown herbs are more environmentally friendly, this will be a big draw card for many customers and as a result good for business.

You can sell your bunches for $1 to $2 for common herbs, more for rarer herb varieties.

234 Design and build water features

Water features create a focal point in a garden and as well as being stylish they provide a lovely calming effect. There are many designs available that are easy to make and can be made from pretty much anything.

You could specialise in water features using recycled materials for a more environmentally friendly option. You could source your materials at garage sales, salvage yards, from junk left on the side of the road or for free by searching newspaper and online classifieds. This would keep your costs down and enable you to create unique water features that double as works of art.

You could make $50 for small water features and hundreds for large features. You could offer installation as well for an extra fee.

235 Become a DIY handyperson

A handyperson can be hired for all the odd jobs, such as replacing doors, tidying the garden, cleaning gutters — all the little things that need to be done but many people can't do. You don't necessarily need certification in any particular aspect of home maintenance, as long as you stick to jobs that don't require specific qualifications, such as electrical work.

You need to be handy with tools and have basic knowledge about home repairs and maintenance. If you don't have your own tools already, you will have to spend a bit before you can begin work.

To get started you can distribute flyers door to door or contact real estate agencies and ask to be put on their books for rental property repairs.

You can make from $50 for small jobs and upwards of $1000 for large jobs.

 ## 236 Fix flyscreens

Many people don't realise that to fix a torn flyscreen you can simply replace the screen instead of the entire frame and screen. You could buy the screen in bulk and offer a screen replacement service, which would be a much cheaper option.

It is relatively easy to do. The hardest part will be accessing high or hard-to-reach windows, but the actual replacing of the screen doesn't take long. You could also combine this service along with other home maintenance or domestic work, such as gardening.

To fix flyscreens you could charge $15 to $20 for an easy-to-reach window and more for hard-to-reach windows.

237   Become a tiler

Tiling is lucrative work if you are good, but if it's not your specialty don't even attempt it. You will need to have a Certificate III in tiling to work in the industry, which you can get from attending a TAFE course. There is a real shortage of good tilers around, and since more people are opting to stay in their current homes and renovate, there is a lot of work available.

Once you are certified you can work for others or start your own business. It will be hard initially as people will want to hire an experienced tiler and to see proof of your work and speak to your referees. To gain references you could offer a discount to your first 10 customers. You can easily make from $500 per job.

238   Work as a school groundskeeper

A school groundskeeper maintains the school grounds, carries out minor repairs, organises larger repairs and so on. This work is usually full time but some schools hire contractors to come in for a half-day's work or for a few days a week to take care of repairs and tidy the lawns and gardens.

You could approach schools directly to find out if they employ a groundskeeper or if they contract the work out. Before you begin you will need to have a background check, and you need to like children, as you will be around them a lot.

For this work you can make $15 to $25 an hour.

Become a caretaker for holiday homes

Caretaking for holiday homes is something many people do for years. You usually live in the guesthouse or nearby. Your duties will include mowing the lawn, maintaining the gardens, cleaning the house and preparing the home for when the owners arrive. Some homes only get visited once a year by their owners, so it can be a great way to get paid to live somewhere while saving for your own place.

These jobs are often found via agencies or online. You will need good references and be willing to live at someone else's home.

You can make from $20 an hour by doing normal home and garden maintenance.

 240 Install electric pool covers

Usually you don't mix electricity and water, but there is a product that is safe — electric pool covers. Many people are having them installed as it is much easier to flick a switch and the pool cover comes on and off, rather than having to wind it yourself.

This sort of business will be more popular in wealthier areas because the residents will be far more likely to own pools and have the money to install covers. And you are likely to get more business after installing just one cover as many of the residents won't like to be outdone by their neighbours.

Your clients will also need to have the covers maintained. Your service could include the maintenance as an extra component, or you could partner with someone where you install the cover and they provide maintenance.

Training on how to install them will be necessary. Once this is complete you can send out flyers or advertise online. You can make from $400 an installation.

241 Replace doors

Door frames and doors often get damaged or shift with the weather and need replacing or refitting. This is a service you could offer with just a few tools, along with a trailer if you need to transport the doors and frames. If you are handy with woodwork, measuring and cutting, the installation won't be too hard.

Some companies have a monopoly on this type of work, but you could make your point of difference your excellent customer service and unique custom doors. It may take a little time to build a reputation, but if you are good, word of mouth will spread quickly.

You can make approximately $300 for a front entrance door, or from $1000 if you do the frames as well.

242 Build retaining walls

Anyone living on sloped land needs retaining walls built for entertainment areas to be levelled off without the land sliding down the slopes and getting everything dirty or just so the garden can actually be used. They can be made from sandstone, rendered brick, wood or even besser blocks. You could offer a few types of service, such as building a single wall, or the wall with a garden.

You will need access to cheap supplies as well as a trailer to transport your tools and supplies to customers' homes. In terms of the actual work, once you know about drainage the construction is relatively simple to do.

How much you charge will depend on the size of the job but you could easily make in excess of $1000.

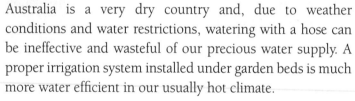

243 Install irrigation systems

Australia is a very dry country and, due to weather conditions and water restrictions, watering with a hose can be ineffective and wasteful of our precious water supply. A proper irrigation system installed under garden beds is much more water efficient in our usually hot climate.

The installation is a big job but it will save customers a lot of money and time, and will ensure their gardens are green and growing properly because they are getting the necessary water.

You will need either a ute or a van to cart your supplies and tools around in. If you already have the right transport, you won't need much money to start up.

You can make from $500 per job depending on the size of the system you are installing.

244 Install grey water systems

People are always looking for ways to be more environmentally friendly and installing a grey water system is an excellent way to do that. They save loads of water being wasted by redirecting it outside to the garden, and more advanced systems even filter and recycle the water; however, these need to be installed by a plumber.

Some councils require approval of grey water projects, so your service could include the applications and processing fees to save your clients the hassle of organising it themselves.

You can choose to set yourself up with some grey water systems or just take information with you when doing a quote for a client and then order the systems when required. You will need a complete tool kit, information on grey water systems and a ute or a car large enough to deliver the systems. Some systems require a plumber to install them, so you need to be aware of which ones you can and can't install yourself.

You can start out distributing flyers and advertising online and in your local newspaper. You can make from $500 depending on the size of the job.

245 Women helping women

Many women find it intimidating to have a man they don't know working in their home, so if you are a confident, competent and handy woman, this could be a great idea for you. You will need to work out your speciality—such as fixing flyscreens, cleaning gutters, unclogging drains, carpentry or replastering—so you can advertise exactly which services you want to provide.

Then with the right transport, such as a ute or a car with a trailer, and a toolkit you will be able to do a variety of jobs. You can advertise using the usual methods, but also make sure you inform all the women you know about your new enterprise as they will be your main customers and will refer you to others.

How much you make will vary from job to job but you could easily average from $30 an hour.

 ## 246 Supply and install smoke detectors

Many people don't know how to install smoke detectors but it is quite simple. You could do this work part time or include it with other services if you already do home maintenance work. Smoke detectors don't take long to install and they are fairly cheap to buy, so you will be charging mainly for the call-out fee.

It is now a legal requirement to have smoke detectors in all rental properties, so you could market yourself to real estate agents, since most landlords don't have the time or desire to do minor work like this themselves.

You could charge from $50 for a call-out fee and then a set price per smoke alarm installation.

247 Paint houses

You don't need a qualification to do house painting but you do need to be good at it. There are many homes that need painting both internally and externally. It gives them a whole new look and is something most people don't have the time to do.

You will need some equipment and it may take a while to build up business, but if you're good word of mouth will spread quickly. The main things you will need are a ladder, various brushes and rollers, an electric sander, overalls, goggles, a mask and a ute or a van to cart everything around in. You can charge from $800 per room.

248 Paint window frames

Window frames often get overlooked but can make such a difference to a home, both inside and out. They can make an exterior look fresher and have more street appeal when selling, and they can make an interior appear more finished.

Window frames can be painted as part of a regular painting business or it can be a service of its own. They are fiddlier to paint than walls, so can take a bit of time. You will need to sand existing paint back, apply putty to holes and prepare the area before even starting to paint, so it's not a quick job.

You could charge $50 per hour plus materials. How much you make varies completely on the size of the windows, the number of windows, how much preparation work is needed and so on.

249 Remodel caravans and buses

When I was a child both of my uncles bought a bus and decked them out as motor homes. They remodelled them according to their individual needs—one for his wife and three kids, the other for his wife and six kids, so very different designs—and then went travelling. You could offer a service where you provide the design and then do the remodelling.

Your clients would need to buy a bus themselves and then give you an idea of what they want. You would draw up the plans and install the necessary items to create their dream motor home. If you are good at carpentry, you could do the installation yourself, or if you have the contacts you could subcontract the installation.

You could make upwards of $500 for the design and thousands of dollars depending on what is installed and how it is done.

250 Install dog and cat doors

Dog and cat doors come in a variety of styles and are handy to have, but not everyone wants to install their own. You could make your own to install or buy ready-made doors to install. As long as you use common sense they don't take long to install.

To get started you could ask vets, pet stores and animal shelters if you can advertise through them or if they will recommend you. You will need some tools but the doors themselves need not be purchased until an order is made, making start-up costs smaller.

You could charge from \$80 to install a door, excluding materials.

251 Install new locks

Installing new door handles is easy enough, but you can't call yourself a locksmith without proper training. To be a qualified locksmith you need to do an apprenticeship as the job entails more than just changing locks. As a handyperson you can change locks on doors and windows, but you can't do everything a locksmith does.

Your service needn't focus on just front and back doors; you could also install simple slide locks for bathrooms or locks on bedroom doors.

You could promote yourself through real estate agents or simply do a flyer drop.

Without proper locksmith training you can't charge as much as the professionals, but you can still charge from \$40, excluding materials.

252 Render house exteriors

Cement rendering can add a lot of value to a home and make it much easier to sell. It can be learnt fairly easily and takes a bit of practice to perfect your technique but there are no specific qualifications needed in Australia to render.

You will need some tools and a few larger items, such as a cement mixer, to make the job easier and faster. Once you are set up contact developers of new properties or owners of older homes to see if they would like to do business with you. You can charge $25 to $40 per square metre.

253 Paint street numbers

Many homes don't indicate their street number on their property. Visible street numbers make it much easier to find a home and look good when done professionally.

You could spray paint the numbers onto the gutter in front of the home, or paint street numbers on the actual house or letterbox. Another option is to paint them on wheelie bins so they are less likely to be stolen and can easily be returned if they do go missing. You can offer different types of lettering or a variety of colours so the client can choose a style that matches their home.

You could charge from $10 per home or offer a discount if numerous homes in the street are done together.

254 Work as a nanny

If you love children, nannying can be an excellent way to travel while maintaining a work history. Many nannies travel the world by working for different families. They do a year in the US, a year in the UK, a year in France, just travelling from country to country. Other nannies get a job with a well-off or famous family and then get to travel with the family when they go on holidays.

Not all nannying jobs are great and the pay can be quite low if you have no qualifications or experience, but your salary will increase the longer you work. You can also be a live-in nanny, which means you don't pay for accommodation, food or household bills but you still get a wage, and this can be a good deal.

To find work you can sign up with online nannying agencies and travel agencies such as STA Travel, which offer programs that combine work and travel, or you can ask friends and family if they know of anyone looking for a nanny.

If you have no nanny certification and you live with the family, the pay can be about $200 per week, but can get much higher depending on your experience and qualifications.

Part VII

MAKE MONEY FROM

YOUR KNOWLEDGE

If you have a special talent or specialised knowledge in a particular area, you can turn that knowledge into a way to make money. If you are good at what you do, you might find yourself getting paid to enjoy your own hobby. This section includes ideas for photographic work right through to consulting and computer assistance.

255 Become a freelance travel photographer

If you love to travel and you are good at taking photos, you could sell them to magazines and websites or print them onto canvases and sell them as framed photos. As a freelancer you won't be tied down to any particular place and no-one can tell you exactly what to photograph. You will need a good camera and some photographic knowledge.

There are many websites you can sell your pictures to, or you could set up your own website and contact magazines to see if they are interested in your work.

You can make from $100 through to thousands of dollars for a photograph.

256 Become a child photographer

Photographing children can be harder than photographing models as kids can have trouble sitting still or holding poses and they are known for tantrums, but it can still be a lot of fun. You could work for agencies or magazines, or work as a freelancer.

If you have a good camera and enjoy working with kids, you could do really well. Outdoor shoots can work particularly well because the kids can play around and have fun while you photograph them.

If you freelance, you can earn more since you won't have to pay a percentage of your fee to an agency, but it can be hard to get started. If you work for an agency, you are still likely to make from $500 for a shoot.

257 Undertake freelance photo-graphy for magazines

Magazines and newspapers always need a variety of images to accompany their features. Many source their images from various photographers and photographic websites instead of holding a shoot for every article.

If there is a subject you have a particular interest in photographing, find a magazine or a publication that deals in that area and arrange to show them your work. After you get published once it will be easier to get more work published.

Freelancing can be a great way to make money from a hobby or it can provide the ideal way to be your own boss and work doing what you love. You can make from $100 a photo.

258 'Trash the dress' photography

'Trash the dress' photo shoots are when a bride wears her wedding dress (or one bought to trash) and it gets ruined. Trashing the dress from splashing through the beach, throwing paint on it, wearing it on a farm or near animals are all fun possibilities.

It is increasingly popular with younger brides or even as a divorce 'celebration'. It's usually done on location and can take a bit to set up but you come away with some amazing photos. It needn't focus on just wedding dresses as you can do formal and graduation 'trashes' too.

To get exposure and interest in your work set up some photo shoots to create a portfolio, and also print a large image to display at wedding expos.

You can charge from $500 for the shoot and a few photos. How much you make will depend on the packages you offer.

259 Photograph sunrises to commemorate a baby's birth

Take a picture of the sunrise every morning as a special memento for people to buy to signify the birth of their baby. You could photograph sunrises from picturesque locations such as beaches or mountains, or simply focus on the sunrise and the horizon from anywhere you like. You could also do sunsets as an option for those babies born in the evenings.

You could sell them online, or contact local hospitals to see if they will allow you to sell them to the new mothers. Also attend baby expos with images and examples of your work to gain exposure.

You could charge from $50 depending on the size of the photo.

260 Photograph family portraits on location

Family portraits taken at the beach, your favourite park or anywhere that has special significance have much more meaning than a regular studio portrait. The family tends to be more relaxed and there are also fewer tantrums from kids, who get to play and be themselves somewhere that is familiar to them.

You can get started with just a camera and a website. Choose a kilometre radius in which you will work and anything outside that radius could incur a surcharge if you are willing to travel further occasionally.

You could charge $100 for the location, and then create packages starting from $250.

261 Photograph pregnancy to birth

You could specialise in photographing pregnancy to birth images and sell them as packages. It could be a complete package, including a selection of tasteful pregnancy photos then some photos of the newborn. Your client can choose at what stages of the pregnancy they prefer to be photographed, such as six or eight months, and how soon after the birth they would like their baby's photos taken.

You will need a studio, some sheets and props, as well as your camera. It is up to you to decide whether you shoot on location or in the studio. You can charge from $750 per package.

262 Photograph food

Many people think food photography couldn't be that hard but there is a certain art to it. There are many possibilities for food photographers, such as working for food magazines and cookbook publishers, photographing images for websites or by creating their own foodie blog.

You can contact publishers with samples of your work, or just set up a blog with your photos and get exposure by linking to other blogs.

How much you make will depend on which method of publication you choose, how well known you are and how much work you are required to do, but you could make from $400 for a simple shoot.

263 Photograph glamour sessions

Photographing glamour sessions is when the client has their hair and make-up done and is photographed. Basically they are made to feel special for the day. Fully dressed glamour or boudoir shoots are becoming increasingly popular.

You will need your client to bring their own clothing if it is a boudoir shoot, but you can provide a variety of clothing and accessories for glamour shots, such as fur or leather.

To get started you can display your work at expos to attract clients. You could also make an arrangement with a gym where you take a glamour shot at the end of a boot camp course as part of a package that they offer to their clients. The clients would be able to receive one photograph at no cost from their shoot with you, with any other photos costing extra.

You can make from $1000 per session. The photos incur an additional fee.

264 Photograph pets

It is amazing how much people spend on their pets. For many people their pets are their children and they pamper them. You could offer photo sessions for the furry members of the family.

Provide items such as bows, spike collars, velvet or silk to be included in the photos, or clients can bring their own items. You could also provide grooming, or request that all animals be photograph ready when they arrive.

To get started contact pet stores, vets and any places that deal with animals to discuss cross-promotion.

You could charge from $100 a session with packages starting at $250.

265 Teach photography

If you are a good photographer, you could teach others how to do it. There are many people around who would love to know more than point and click. Depending on which style you wish to teach, you could offer a night class with a community college, or teach from your own home or on location at parks and beaches.

Teaching a night class is a great way to get started and then you can branch out and do it yourself anywhere. Once you gain a reputation or some repeat students for more advanced classes you could raise your prices (keeping in mind that the college will take a percentage of your fees). You could charge from $200 per student for 10 lessons.

266 Sell your photos online

U18

There are a variety of online photographic websites where you can upload your photos and get paid when people use them or want to buy them. The pay is often quite small but all you need to do is upload your images. The website then processes the payments and pays you, so it is hassle-free money.

Search online for photo websites and then read reviews about them to get an idea of whether they are legitimate or not. Then all you need to do is take some interesting photos, sign up and upload them to the website and tag your pictures. They will sit there forever and can be downloaded and paid for numerous times over.

You can make from as little as $1 a photo right up to hundreds of dollars.

267 Set up electrical equipment

If you are good at setting up electrical equipment, this is a service that many people require as technology gets more and more advanced and confusing. All you need is a few tools and knowledge about electrical set-ups. Most of the time the jobs won't be difficult but many people won't even want to attempt to do it themselves.

Contact electrical goods stores to see if they will refer you to their customers. You could arrange to be paid a percentage of the sale in return for a flat referral fee. You can make from $100 for call out and a simple set-up.

268 Assemble furniture

Not everyone is good at putting together furniture. Or they think they can do it and then give up, leaving the unassembled furniture in an unusable state. Armed with just an Allen key and a little bit of handy know-how you can easily set up flat-pack furniture.

To get started contact stores that sell flat-pack furniture and ask if they will refer you, or arrange a deal where you do set-ups for them for a fee. Removalists are another good business you could get referrals through.

You could charge $50 per call out, plus an hourly rate for the assembly or a per job rate.

269 Set up computers

Most people are lost when it comes to computers, so if you know what you are doing, you could make a nice little business out of setting up computers. They are often more complex than other electrical items and cause many people to scream in frustration. Since computers are usually not cheap, it is better for most people to pay a little extra to have someone who knows what they are doing set it up for them.

Most of your business will probably come from word of mouth or referrals, or you could contact computer stores and make an arrangement with them. You could charge from $100 for a set-up.

270 Teach basic computer programs

Many people lack confidence when using new computer programs. A basic understanding of Microsoft Works or Quicken is often required for administration roles and it is something that can be taught relatively easily.

You could teach classes at a community college or contact computing stores and ask to be referred when people purchase a computer. You could also contact businesses with administration roles and offer your services to train their staff.

At community colleges you could charge from $150 for 10 lessons, or for private lessons you could charge $30 per hour.

271 Become a green consultant

A green consultant is someone who shows people how to create environmentally friendly homes. You could charge your clients a fee to do a green consultation, as well as make arrangements with businesses to get a percentage of sales from any business you send their way, such as rainwater tanks or cloth nappy suppliers. You will need to ensure they do good work before recommending them.

You can attend green expos to get exposure, or offer to do a free consultation in a more affluent area, then let your business grow from word of mouth recommendations. You could also contact magazines or newspapers to see if they are interested in writing a feature about your work.

You could charge $50 to $200 per consultation.

 272 Offer your services as a wardrobe consultant

Some people are no good at selecting outfits and really need someone to show them what to wear. You could either do a consultation in their home using their clothing and then create a list of items they could buy to complement what they already have, or you could take them shopping to buy a whole new wardrobe and get rid of everything else.

If you take them shopping, the consultation will take longer and you can charge accordingly. You might also be able to make arrangements with certain shops for your clients to receive discounts, making them more likely to buy there.

You could charge $300 for a short in-home consultation, or from $600 for a longer consultation including shopping.

 273 Become a creative space consultant

You could advise your clients on how to make the best use of their homes by showing them creative solutions for utilising more space, possibly by converting some furniture they already own into storage items, or showing them great products that would help them.

With the cost of houses rising, many people are preferring to buy smaller homes or are staying in a home they bought years ago that is now bursting at the seams. You just need a bit of creative flair and an eye for creating space. It is a bonus if you have personal experience in small space living.

You can charge from $100 for a short consultation, more if you provide designs where clients can convert their furniture.

274 Organise reunions

Many people like the idea of a family or school reunion but never get around to doing it because of the effort it would take to organise. This is where you step in. All you would need is the list of people to be invited and if possible their last-known addresses so you can find them all.

You could also book the venue and organise catering, invitations and anything else required, so it is as stress-free as possible for all involved.

You could charge from $600 for finding everyone if it is a large group to over $1000 if you organise the entire event, including entertainment and food.

275 Become a survival skills consultant

Thanks to various TV shows many people are fascinated by survival skills. You could run camps teaching people how to survive on the land, showing them how to make a fire, which plants are safe to eat, how to create a shelter and so on.

If you have acreage, you could do it on your own land, otherwise you could hire a spot and run the camps from there. You could teach simple survival skills where people can bring a few creature comforts, such as sleeping mats and some food, right through to extreme survival skills where they come with nothing and have to find everything from food and water to shelter and how to create signals so you can be found.

You could charge from $200 for overnight camps or from $600 for camps of a few days.

 276 Prepare homes for sale

Many people have no idea about the little things they can do to increase the value of their home or how they should present it to get the best possible price when putting it on the market. If you have some creative flair and a good decorating eye, along with some knowledge about selling homes, you could specialise in this service.

I can guarantee that you would be much more helpful than most agents, who want to get the house on the market as quickly as possible, so won't be recommending doing anything that might delay it from getting on the market, even if it means attracting a much higher price.

Your service would be impartial and would provide creative solutions according to the specific budgets and allowable time frames, from repositioning furniture and removing personal objects to hiring completely different furniture and artwork for the duration of the sale, all to make selling easier and more profitable for the seller. You can charge from $800 for this service.

277 Become an antiques personal shopper

Many people love antiques, but have no idea how to tell if an item is a genuine antique or a fake. If you find some shops that stock genuine antiques, you could organise antique shopping tours with groups or offer them one on one. Alternatively, you could hunt down specific items for clients for a set fee.

When conducting tour groups you can offer advice on what to look for when shopping for antiques and show them the stores you use. When taking a client on their own you can tailor a session to suit their interests and provide them with information specific to what they wish to buy or collect.

If you are hunting down specific items for clients who already know what they want, you just have to do the grunt work of finding the item.

You could charge $60 per person for shopping tours and $150 for two hours of one-on-one shopping. For sourcing specific items, charge according to the level of difficulty.

278 Offer your services as a dating consultant

Dating consultants can do a variety of things. They can set up an actual agency or an online website that connects people. Alternatively you could specialise in planning dates for people, including the event or activity, restaurant booking and car service.

If you run an agency, you will need office space, while if you run it online, you will need a good website. As a reputable agency you will have to thoroughly check anyone who wants to join and will try to properly match people.

If you decide to offer a date planning service, clients could contact you with their interests, or how they want the date planned along with their budget and you would then arrange suitable options.

You will more likely be able to arrange better prices for the services that you choose to use as a selling point for your business. Alternatively, use the prices for those services to make up your fee, making your service appear 'free'.

You could charge $40 to organise and plan the date, or keep the discounts. If you have a website that just connects people, you can charge a sign-up fee of $10 or more as well as make money from advertising on your site.

279 Assist with dating preparation

There are many reasons why adults are unsure about getting back into the dating scene, such as being recently widowed, divorced or just having ended a long-term relationship.

You could offer a session that goes over the basics about what has changed since they last began dating, so they know what their dates will expect of them, what will make them stand out and what not to do.

You could offer an extra service to assist them with clothing, accessories and make-up or hair to modernise their appearance.

You could run sessions from your home or as a community college class. You could charge $80 for an evening class held over a few weeks or offer private sessions from $100.

280 Facilitate speed dating

Speed dating is an event where you spend one to two minutes with a person talking about yourself, then they do the same, then you switch tables and do it all over again, potentially meeting up to 15 people in one night. You could organise speed dating events at various venues yourself.

If you want to do it completely on your own, you will need to hire the venues; otherwise you could contact various clubs to see if they are interested in running the event at their venue, with you facilitating. They would get a percentage of the entry fee, plus drink sales to a guaranteed number of people.

It would be an ideal weeknight event for many venues because those nights are slower, and for your guests it would means that they might find someone they like and can then have a follow-up real date on the weekend. You can charge $25 to $45 per person, including one drink.

281 Offer your services as a frugal living consultant

When people need to cut back on their spending many have no idea where they are going wrong and where to start. They choose to keep spending instead and end up deeper and deeper in debt.

You could offer an in-home service where you assess the running of their household and assist them with changing their habits to save them money. You could also offer a daily or weekly email outlining specific tips they could focus on for the week.

Keeping it simple and working with clients in their own home is less daunting for them and more likely to be effective. You could charge $50 for a one-hour consultation.

282   Become a feng shui consultant

To be a true feng shui consultant you need to study it — there are actual feng shui masters who have studied for years. The service you could provide would be to go to people's homes and advise them on how to create the best feng shui by using furniture placement, such as what to place where to counteract negative flow, and by bringing in various items like wind chimes to attract positive flow.

There are many courses available in various forms of feng shui; some run for less than a week while others are longer. Once you are qualified contact natural therapists, real estate agents, health food shops and other businesses that could refer you to their customers or clients.

You can charge from $80 for a simple consultation right through to in excess of $400 for a house design consultation.

283   Offer your services as a head lice consultant

This might sound a little out there, but lice are everywhere and most people don't want to deal with it. You could offer a service where you treat the lice (that is, you are the one who combs through the hair to get rid of them).

You can choose to treat lice with chemicals or offer an all-natural alternative. Not only will you come and treat the lice, you can do a re-treat seven days later to break the cycle, and also offer products to help prevent lice.

You could contact schools, childcare centres and hair salons to see if they will refer you. Anywhere mothers or children go is the best place to advertise. You can charge from $80 for your services.

284 Become a marriage consultant

If you are a properly trained counsellor, you could work as a marriage consultant offering pre-wedding counselling as well as post-wedding counselling. You can offer group classes or one-on-one sessions, or a combination of both.

Couples often focus more on the big day than their actual marriage when planning their wedding, so a pre-wedding consultation along with some counselling is an excellent way to ensure the happy couple starts off on the right foot. You might like to include conflict resolution in your counselling, as this often gets glossed over but is very important.

You can contact churches, registry offices, bridal stores and anywhere that deals with weddings to ask if they will recommend your services.

You can create a variety of packages from a single consultation for $80 to a few consultations for a package price.

285 Work as a weight-loss consultant

Weight is a huge issue for many people, and people are getting bigger and bigger despite the numerous weight-loss products and services available.

Rather than just supply dietary meals or offer personal training, you could do a weekly weigh in for your clients, with a motivational daily call or email, as well set them up with a gym membership or teach them how to use simple objects at home to exercise with. You can offer shakes and dietary supplements if you like, but most people need to learn actual healthy living.

You could visit clients in their homes and work out their needs and wants and then create a plan for them to lose the desired weight. You could charge from $50 for the initial consultation and from $20 a week for the phone calls and weigh ins.

286 Facilitate VIP nights

Many businesses host VIP nights for their important clients. Every few months an invitation will be sent to the clients for a special evening where they receive discounts, freebies, light refreshments and the opportunity to be the first to try new products. A VIP night can boost a business's bottom line and help bring old clients or customers back.

As the organiser of these events your role would be to secure a discounted price for everything required on the night, organise and send out the invitations and do everything necessary to ensure that the event runs smoothly. To get the number of clients you need, you can stress that there are limited spaces so the event is strictly RSVP.

After you have hosted these events regularly you will have built up a good contacts list from catering services, venue hire and sample bags to printing needs such as invitations and thankyou cards.

You can charge from $400 for your services, excluding catering and other costs.

287 Offer your services as a musical consultant

Not all businesses realise the effect that music can have on their customers, clients and staff. You could consult with businesses about their aims and the role background music can play, then compile CDs specific to their business.

Large department stores and supermarkets are already aware of this and play music accordingly to make you browse more slowly and increase your desire to spend. Other places such as bus and train stations don't want people to loiter so they play music to deter this behaviour.

After researching the music being played at all the businesses in your local area, you could contact them and present them with a package to increase sales with a music makeover. You could charge $65 for a short consultation and a CD.

288 Teach a bushfire-ready course

In recent years we have witnessed an increase in horrific bushfires due to hot, dry and windy conditions. Surprisingly, many people are still not prepared for a bushfire in their area. Many think that it won't happen where they live, but it can happen virtually anywhere.

Your job could be to go to people's homes and show them what they need to do to be ready in case of fire. You could cover things such as cleaning out drains and gutters, removing clutter from around the home, cutting back trees close to their property and keeping the area moist.

You can leave them with a plan of their house, areas that need to be worked on, an evacuation plan and details on how to do it all. You could charge from $80 for this service.

289 Become an emergency plan consultant

As an emergency plan consultant you can teach people how to prepare and what to do in case of a natural disaster, such as a fire, flood, storm or cyclone, both at home and if they are travelling overseas. You could also cover what to do in case of a terrorist attack, mugging and car breakdowns.

Your sessions could be taught as a community college course over a few weeks with a different disaster to be covered each week. Alternatively, you could visit people in their homes and give them more specific advice tailored to their situation and property.

You could charge $150 for a 10-week course, or from $100 for one in-home consultation.

290 Offer your services as a cleaning consultant

Some people have no idea where to start when cleaning their homes. What to do, how to do it, how often things should be cleaned and what actually constitutes 'clean'. Your clients could include anyone who has never had to do any cleaning before, such as students living away from home and young people who have just moved out to recent divorcees.

You could teach them how to clean everything by making them do it alongside you, including which cleaning products are best for which job, how to get stains out of clothing, and which cleaning products you can make yourself to save money and be more environmentally friendly.

You could advertise at colleges if you want to target students and young adults, or do a letterbox drop or advertise in your local newspaper if you want to focus on divorcees instead. You could charge $50 for a one-hour consultation.

291 Become a business coach

Being a business coach is one of those professions that sound a bit vague but if done well can be extremely beneficial for businesses. Your role is to analyse every area of the business and how it can be improved, or you could help businesses when they are starting up.

You will need to provide clear details about how you can improve productivity, profits, staff morale and so on. A background in marketing and business helps, but is not essential. If you have a creative and analytical mind and can see the gaps in a business and can offer strategies to set them straight, you would be great in this role.

You can work out a variety of packages tailored to different businesses and then approach them outlining what you have to offer. Your packages could start at $500 for the basics and go for thousands of dollars for more in-depth coaching.

292 Teach how to market a business

Some businesses can't afford a huge marketing budget so it's difficult for them to stay ahead of the competition. You could step in and show them low-cost solutions, such as how to advertise cheaply or for free and how to maintain client relationships, simple things that can make a big difference to a business.

You could create a budget package to present to businesses and then approach those in your local community or who you think could use your services. If you create a good group of clients, you could create an excellent cross-promotion circle that could benefit them all. A small budget package could start at $200.

293 Become a life coach

Life coaches can help people overhaul their lives. By inspiring and motivating their clients, a life coach can help people handle their finances better, lose weight, get healthier—the possibilities are endless.

You can do this work face to face by meeting with your clients directly or work with them online. Having a background in counselling, therapeutic work or business helps, but there is no real qualification necessary for life coaching. You do need to be naturally happy, outgoing and confident to be able to motivate others, though.

To attract clients you could arrange with gyms to be included in their membership packages, with a percentage of your fee going to the gym, or contact businesses such as hair and beauty salons and offer a deal to bring clients to them in exchange for them recommending you.

You can charge depending on the type of service you provide and your location; life coaches in larger cities can usually charge more. For example, you can charge $50 to $100 for a one-hour phone call, $200 to $400 for a one-hour individual session and $250 to $450 for a one-hour face-to-face group session. Packages are often created for one to two sessions per week for three months, equating to $3250 to $6500 per client.

294 Become a financial planner

You need qualifications to work as a financial planner, but it is a great job. You can work your own hours and charge a fee, or collect fees from the products you recommend instead of charging your client. You can do it from home, visit clients in their homes or work for a company.

You can get qualified at your own pace through online distance education or you can go to school. Both your studies and your job can be worked around kids easily.

Once you are qualified, if you want to work for yourself contact other businesses in a similar field to see if they will refer you. If you specialise in mortgages, contact real estate agencies and ask if you can be present at open home inspections to hand out your card and set up meetings with prospective buyers. On average you can make $80 000 to $120 000 a year.

295 Teach how to invest in the stock market

Many people like the idea of owning shares but don't know how to buy them. You could teach everything from how to choose a stockbroker to doing it yourself by picking stocks, buying and selling, 'reading' the market and so on. You can also help people work out their risk level and whether they are comfortable investing in stocks.

There is so much involved and it can be overwhelming for many people, so anything from a class or seminar to a one-on-one private consultation would be possible. You could offer classes through a community college, or do them privately and promote yourself through flyers and newspapers.

You can make from $300 per person for a seminar or from $50 for a one-hour private consultation.

296 Teach a retirement preparation course

Most people don't realise how low their superannuation will be if relying solely on employer contributions and just how hard it will be to live on the pension when they retire. Many people also don't think beyond the travel and opportunities they will have to relax once they finish work. But what if they live for another 30 or 40 years and need to go into a retirement home? What happens if they need to give power of attorney to someone? How do they organise a will? How can they get retiree discounts? There is so much to consider and attending a course explaining all of this at any stage in your life would be very useful.

You could teach this course through a community college or as a wealth seminar. You needn't be a financial planner or give specific financial advice, as you could focus on what needs to be done and how to live as a retiree instead of how to invest.

You could charge from $150 for a community college course; more if you are offering it as a wealth seminar or if you are a qualified financial planner.

297 Write a retirement preparation ebook

A retirement preparation ebook could be sold on your blog or website, or through someone else's and they get commission for selling it. It could include everything a retirement planning course might, such as organising a will, how to choose a retirement home and how to get retiree discounts.

It would be simple to put together—the hardest part would be marketing it. One of the easiest ways to get it out there would be to contact financial bloggers and offer them an affiliate package if they do a feature on your ebook and offer it for sale on their website. You can also try selling it on the websites of large bookshops.

It is up to you how much you charge for your ebook, how much you give to your affiliates and how often you pay them. Many ebooks sell from $4.95 to $19.95.

298 Become a mortgage broker

The number of mortgage options out there makes it very confusing for the average consumer. Your role as a mortgage broker is to find the right home loan to suit their financial situation. You need proper qualifications to become a mortgage broker, but it is a very flexible occupation. You can work for yourself and visit clients in their homes, or you can work for a company specialising in mortgage broking or a bank.

To get experience you could work directly for a company and then branch out on your own if you like. There are many mortgage broking companies that allow you to work as a contractor and choose your own hours anyway, so it is very similar to doing it yourself. You can make in excess of $75 000 a year.

299 Become a freelance travel journalist

To work as a freelance travel journalist you don't need to be qualified as a journalist but it helps a lot. You must have good communication skills and be able to write interesting easy-to-read articles.

As a freelancer you don't work for anyone specifically, which can make it both easier and harder. You can choose how much to sell your work for and what you want to write about, or you can select the jobs you would like to do. It can be hard to get started and establish a name in the industry.

To get your name out there you could write articles and submit them to online forums, blogs, eZines and a variety of other online sources. It is a competitive industry, but if you are good and market your work well, you will find work.

You can make $25 to $300 per article when starting out but much more once you are successful.

Teach interview skills

Many people are simply not good at being interviewed or get extremely nervous during interviews. You could train people to improve their interview skills by teaching them how to answer questions clearly and intelligently and to stay calm during an interview, how to manage a group interview and how to dress for success.

You could offer your sessions as a community college course, or contact businesses similar to yours such as résumé writers and employment agencies to get referrals. Offer a few clients a free session to get started and to get a reputation, then ask that they provide testimonials for you if they get the job.

You can charge from $150 for a few hours of training, which can be done over the phone or face to face.

301 Maintain bicycles

It's not just cars and motorbikes that need to be serviced and fixed—bicycles need to, too. You could offer a mobile service as an alternative to customers having to take their bike into a shop; you could go to customers' homes and fix the bike there, or pick it up and drop it off once your work is done.

You will need some tools and a few things such as lubricant and grease, as well as a puncture repair kit. You will need to source companies that sell bike parts such as tyres and inner tubes cheaply so you can make a decent income.

You can charge anything from $30 to $150 per bike service, depending on what is required.

  302 Sell motors for petrol—powered bicycles

Petrol-powered bicycles are much cheaper to run than a car or motorbike and are easier to ride than a regular bike. They use small petrol motors and often have very little servicing needs in comparison to a motorbike. They are excellent for those who don't want the expense of a second car but live too far away to cycle to work or do shift work.

You could sell these motors and people could install them on their own bikes, or you could sell the bikes with the motor already attached. In some Australian states the bike needs to be registered before a motor is attached, so that is something you should check first.

You could sell them online, or contact bike stores to see if they are interested in stocking them or referring customers to you. The engines could sell from $200, and a complete engine and bike from $600.

303 Offer your services as a baby shopper

Looking at all the products out there for babies can be overwhelming for parents-to-be and not everyone lives near family or has people close by who can show them what they need. You could help people purchase items for their new baby.

You could have a consultation with them to discuss what their needs are for setting up a nursery and the various other equipment their baby will require, such as a pram and car seat, and then help them find the right items. You could make arrangements with various baby stores to get discounts for your clients in exchange for shopping there.

You could advertise through parenting websites and forums, parenting and pregnancy magazines, baby shops and baby expos. You could charge from $100 for a few hours.

304 Offer search engine optimisation to companies and websites

Search engine optimisation (SEO) is when websites use particular words or phrases to make themselves more attractive to search engines, such as Google, which in turn gives the websites higher rankings. You don't need a qualification to do this work but you do need more than a basic knowledge of it to do it successfully. If not done well, a search engine will recognise a website as spam or as nothing much at all, but if optimised properly, it can be extremely beneficial for a website.

To gain experience you can start by doing this yourself from home by setting up your own website and promoting yourself on other websites and forums and other work-at-home or working parent groups. You can charge from $500 for this service.

305 Teach search engine optimisation

If you are an SEO expert, you could offer to teach others how to do it as well as do it for them. You could teach it as a community college class or through private consultations. Alternatively, you could write an ebook that covers the lessons and accompanies the actual training, or sell the ebook on its own instead of doing consultations.

To make yourself known, set up a website and then promote it on other sites and forums, with a link back to your website offering advice or requesting that they contact you for further help. This way your link is always out there and you have proven how helpful you are.

You can charge from $200 for a two-to-three-hour consultation.

306 Become a family historian

Many people are becoming interested in their family history. You could run a service that teaches people how to use online family history programs or you could provide a service where you do the search for them; however, most people want to find out how to do it themselves because they find out such amazing things along the way.

You could work from an office where clients come to you, or you could visit them at their home. Advertising on family history websites and forums would be a good way to get business. Running a short course through a community college for eight to 10 weeks would also attract interest.

You can charge from $30 per hour for a consultation or offer short courses for a few hundred dollars.

Sell swords

Importing and selling swords or knives in most areas requires a licence of some sort. If you have a few overseas contacts, you could import and sell more unique knives. To check the requirements in Australia simply call customs and they can inform you if what you would like to sell is legal or not.

Once you are set up you could sell directly online, or contact stores such as tobacconists, gothic stores, and weapon and hunting stores to ask if they will stock your swords. There are many items that are illegal, so ensure you research thoroughly beforehand.

You can make $10 to $50 by selling more common swords and upwards of $200 for more intricate and unique swords.

308 Put on an art exhibit

You don't have to be exhibiting your own work to put on an art exhibit; you could exhibit the work of a collection of artists with a similar theme. You don't have to hold it in a gallery either, it could be done anywhere you can hang or display art and reasonably section off.

You could charge an entry fee and provide some refreshments, which can possibly be sourced from a local vineyard and cafe for a discount or for free as they will attract publicity from their food and wine.

Once you have a location you can advertise for artists through art schools, universities or local galleries. When you have enough artworks to exhibit, advertise the exhibition in newspapers, art publications, online, through the artists themselves and anywhere appropriate. You can charge from $20 a ticket, more for better known artists.

309 Host an art and craft show

Hosting an art and craft show is a big task, but you can reap significant rewards. You will need to scout locations and find people interested in having a stall or demonstrating crafts at the show.

You could offer a variety of classes that people can choose to pay extra to join, as well as stalls of items for sale from quilts to craft supplies. You could have a kids section where parents can leave their kids to do arts and crafts for a little while and parents can browse.

You could advertise through craft magazines and websites, or offer tickets to give away on craft blogs. You could charge an entry fee of $3 to $10, plus a stall holders' fee of $20 to $50, a fee for the kids section of $2 to $5 and adult classes could cost around $30 to $50 a class.

Part VIII

MAKE MONEY WITH BEAUTY

Not all of the ideas in this section require you to have a qualification but for most of them you do need either a hairdressing or beauty certificate. Whereas in the past you needed to complete a four-year apprenticeship, the good news is that you can now get either of these qualifications much faster.

Some of these ideas require a bit of money to get started, but if you are smart about how you spend your money and can find good suppliers, you can make money before you spend any.

3 1 0   Become a make-up artist

As a make-up artist you can work for a store or a salon or have your own mobile business. There is work available with agencies, for film, TV and theatre, or for bridal and formal events.

You can become qualified either on the job by working with other make-up artists, by doing a course through TAFE, or by attending a make-up college where you will also be taught theatrical and special effects make-up.

To get your own business started, create a portfolio, get signage for your car and then contact businesses that might be interested in cross-promotion.

You can charge from around $100 for wedding make-up, or as an hourly rate for theatrical productions.

3 1 1   Work as an updo stylist

As an updo stylist you would normally be a qualified hairdresser that focuses on wedding and special occasion hair. You could combine this work with make-up for an all-in-one service.

You will need some equipment, such as a hair dryer and straightener, as well as bobby pins, hair ties and a variety of brushes, combs and hair products. You will need to create a portfolio of your work to show potential customers, which you can do by using a few friends as models.

If you are interested in doing mostly wedding hair, you can attend bridal expos or advertise through bridal magazines and websites. You can charge from $80 an updo.

312 Become a mobile hairdresser

A mobile hairdresser is very popular with the elderly, those who have injuries or those with young children, as it is harder to leave the home to look after their hair. You could select which services you offer, such as cuts, colouring and blow-dries. You will save by not having to pay rent for premises, but you will need to pay for petrol costs, which can be built into your fee. You can decide the hours you work—after hours is great for parents as they can have their hair done when the other parent comes home from work.

You will first need to register your business name and apply for an Australian business number (ABN) and then you can advertise; in most areas you won't need council permission as you won't be based in one location.

You won't need a large car or van to store your equipment, but you will need a system to hold all of your products and equipment. Most portable equipment can be folded up to fit easily in a car.

How much you make is up to you, but you can charge from $25 for cuts and from $70 for colouring.

313 Work as a mobile beautician

A mobile beautician is much the same as a mobile hairdresser; you are just offering a different service. You will need to qualify as a beautician before you can offer your services otherwise you won't be able to get insurance.

You can select which services you offer, such as waxing, manicures, pedicures, facials, massages and body wraps. You could create a spa experience in people's homes or stick to the basic maintenance-type beauty.

You will need to get supplies to start and organise signage for your car. A portable beauty or massage table is very handy and essential if you are doing massages.

You can have a minimum service requirement so you don't end up just doing eyebrow waxes and making no money. As a guide you could charge from $20 for small waxing, from $50 for various massages and from $100 for special occasion make-up, but check the prices in your local area.

314 Make your own line of hair and beauty products

Many people have made their own line of beauty products when they have been unable to find a suitable product for themselves. You could create environmentally friendly products, specialise in organic and fair trade products, or just create products with scents you love. You can make anything from shampoo and conditioner to body scrubs and lotions to cosmetics and perfumes.

You can get started in your own kitchen and sell to friends and family. Check the health and legal requirements in your area before starting, though. You can then sell through a party plan, online and at markets, or from unique boutiques and small stores. When you create something you love get it patented so no one can copy it and it will officially be yours. You could easily make $3 to $10 from each product sold.

3 1 5 Massage from home

By setting up a room with a massage table, some soft music, oils and towels you can begin offering a massage service from your own home, choosing your own hours.

You will need to be qualified before you touch anyone or you can do serious damage. You will also need to get council approval to run a business from home; the requirements vary from council to council, but you can still easily make money this way.

Once you are set up, contact similar businesses for cross-promotion, such as mobile hairdressers, natural therapists and health stores. Also contact businesses that do manual labour as their workers often get sore and would benefit from a massage. You can charge from $40 for a half-hour massage or from $70 for one hour.

3 1 6 Offer a mobile massage service

Once you are qualified in massage you could offer a mobile business. You could go to offices, clubs or people's homes. You could even visit patients in hospital or women who have just given birth.

You would need a massage table, towels and oils, but it would be fairly simple to set up, especially as you are unlikely to need council approval, just a business name and an ABN.

You could get started by contacting doctors, hospitals, hair salons or businesses where you offer mini massages, basically anywhere your services might be desired. You could charge from $40 for a half-hour massage or $80 for one hour.

317 Work in sports massage

You can provide sports massages either for sports clubs and be at every game, or offer your service to relieve injuries aggravated during the week and to promote healing. The hours are unusual as you will be working around sporting events, but this is a rewarding career. You need to be qualified in sports massage, as you will be treating muscular pain and this is a more in-depth type of massage.

Contact clubs to see if they are interested in hiring you. You can offer to do away games as well as home games so players can be treated immediately when the need arises, as well as after matches so they are not travelling home sore.

You can make from $800 per week depending on your experience and where you are working. You will earn less if you work for a private practice rather than for a sports club.

318 Provide mini massages

Mini massages are ideal for many workplaces. They reduce the risk of repetitive strain injury (RSI) and improve productivity. You could go to various workplaces and give a five-minute neck and shoulder massage for each staff member at a set rate for the company.

Contact the businesses directly outlining what you do and the proven benefits for the company. Alternatively, you could set up at a market or in a very small space in a shopping centre and offer five- to 10-minute massages for a fee. Just set up a sign, your table and a privacy screen.

You can make from $80 an hour at a workplace, or $10 for a five-minute massage at a market.

  ### 319 *offer maternity massage*

 Many women ache all over during pregnancy but there are many massages that are not suitable for pregnant women. You could buy a proper chair for pregnancy massages and specialise in easing aches and pains. You could also offer a labour-inducing massage for those mothers who are overdue, but as long as it is done with care. Another option is to teach infancy massage to mothers to promote bonding with their newborn baby.

You could do this from home, at markets, or rent a room in a salon and do it from there. You could advertise in magazines, at baby and kids markets, by distributing flyers or as a special offer with Bounty Bags <www.bountybags.com.au>. Another option is to advertise at The Baby and Toddler Show <www.babyandtoddlershow.com.au>, an event held in Melbourne, Sydney, Perth and Brisbane. You could charge $40 for a half-hour massage.

320 *whiten teeth*

Teeth whitening improves people's confidence and their looks. You could offer this service in conjunction with your own hair or beauty businesses, or on its own. You could also work as a consultant who comes in on certain days for other salons or businesses.

Many teeth whitening products don't require qualifications to use. You will need to find the teeth whitening product you like, create a portfolio by taking images of clients who have had success with you and contact businesses to find work opportunities.

Besides offering the teeth whitening service yourself, you could also sell the product to other beauty businesses. You can charge from $700 for the service or make more money by selling the product.

321 Offer a tanning bed service

Tanning beds are not as popular as they used to be due to the UV rays and cancer possibilities involved, but there are still many people who prefer to use this method instead of having a spray tan and there is less risk of the colour not being right.

You could have a bed set up in your home or rent them to beauty salons. Clients will need to be made aware of the risks associated with using a tanning bed and will be required to sign waivers to protect you from future law suits.

You can charge from $10 for a casual visit or sell packs of 10 sessions from $80.

322 Offer mobile spray tans

If done properly, spray tans can look great. If done badly, they can look terrible. However, spray tanning is easy to learn and cheap to set yourself up, and it is becoming extremely popular due to the risks associated with solariums and sunbaking.

You can offer spray tanning as a mobile business using the spray tanning machine, your tanning solution, towels, disposable underwear and a pop up tent. To get experience, practise on your friends and family, then get some signage on your car and distribute flyers.

You can charge from $25 for a half body and from $50 for full body. For customers who wish to maintain their tan you can offer discounts if they redo a tan within seven to 10 days.

 ## 323 Become a tattoo artist

Becoming a tattoo artist is not as easy as many people think. You can buy kits and teach yourself, but who would be willing to let you practise on them?

You need to be naturally good at art and have a portfolio of your designs. You need to then find someone willing to mentor and teach you. This can be the hardest part. If you decide to teach yourself, make sure you get a lot of practice before charging clients.

You will need to buy a machine and inks as well as sterile items, such as needles, and will need to know what needs to be thrown out after use, how to clean everything, and all the proper health and safety regulations.

You can charge $50 for small basic tattoos up to hundreds of dollars for more intricate works. Your fees should be based on the length of time the tattoo takes, not on the size of the tattoo.

324 Offer ear piercing

Ear piercing is relatively easy once you know how to do it. You'll need a bit of practice to start with, but it doesn't take too long to learn. There are short courses you can take or you can simply learn on the job.

Once you are qualified you could do it part time from home or get a job at a beauty salon or even a pharmacy. You could have a stand at markets and do piercings there.

Ear piercing on its own won't make a lot of money (you can change about $20), but there are certain things you can do to make your service more attractive to customers. Some cultures and many mothers like their very young children, even babies, to have their ears pierced and you could specialise in working with this age range. This work requires more skill and a lot of patience because children of such a young age move around much more than older people.

325 Become a body piercer

Since some people want every body part pierced, why not make some money from it? Belly, brow and tongue are still the most popular body parts to pierce and you can purchase these rings in bulk from overseas very cheaply.

A qualification is required for body piercing because so much can go wrong if the piercing isn't done correctly. You will need to know where different muscles and ligaments sit, as well as proper health and safety practices.

You could get a job at a beauty salon, piercing and tattoo parlour, or do it as your own business. You could charge from $80 for most body piercings.

 326 Apply make-up on corpses

Applying make-up on corpses to make them look more like themselves for viewings is a common part of a funeral package but not all funeral homes have professionals available to do it, so it doesn't always look right.

You could start your own private business and offer your services to funeral homes, which could hire you to come in and apply the make-up professionally. Otherwise you could be hired directly by the family or friends of the family to do it. You will need a portfolio, which might not be easy to obtain, showing before and after shots. You can make from $80 for each client.

 327 Host pamper parties

Pamper parties can be hosted in a few ways. You could offer them as a consultant with a party plan or you could simply teach others how to do their own manicures and pedicures. They could be promoted as a fun girls' night in, part of pre-wedding preparations or for birthday parties, especially for teens who aren't sure how to do it all.

You could supply everything, show them how to apply and use the products, and then they could take turns doing it for each other. If you want to take an environmentally friendly route, you could do pamper parties using natural ingredients and show people how to treat themselves with items they probably have in their own pantries.

You could advertise in magazines, online or offer incentives for anyone who books a party from a party. You can make from $100 a party (unless it is through a party plan), as well as any sales from selling products.

328 Provide a post-labour glam service

Your business could specialise in making new mums feel better after labour. You could come in after the birth, do the mother's hair and make-up, possibly a quick manicure as well, to help her feel fresh and gorgeous before all the family rushes in and takes photos of her with her new-born.

You would need a hair dryer, a few brushes and other hair products and supplies, as well as make-up (or request that they supply their own so they look more like themselves) and any products for other beauty services you may provide. Your hours will need to be flexible, but ensure that you have some set hours so it doesn't become a 24-hour job.

You could contact midwives, obstetricians, hospitals and birthing centres to see if you can distribute flyers promoting your services. You could charge from $150 for your services.

329 Teach grooming and deportment

Proper manners and grooming don't seem all that necessary to younger generations but as they get older and start seeking employment they quickly realise how important they are. With a background in etiquette or modelling you could teach grooming and deportment classes. They could be done through a community college or you could contact schools to see if they are interested in your services.

Contact modelling agencies, which often provide these classes, to enquire if you could get a job teaching new models. You could also contact employment agencies and present your service as a way for their clients to improve job prospects. You could charge from $100 for a class that covers all the basics.

330 Offer after-hours beauty

Many people are working longer and just can't get to a salon during opening hours. A salon that is open late every night instead of during the day would be very popular among working professionals.

You could offer a service that opens late and finishes late. Provided you have the relevant qualifications you could offer both hair and beauty services or employ people who have the necessary qualifications to work for you.

You could advertise though flyers, newspapers, beauty magazines and online, but many clients will probably notice you by just passing by. Make sure your opening hours are printed on your salon window or door so people can see at any time of day when you are open. You can charge a slightly higher price for working irregular hours, making a basic haircut from $50.

331 Offer an in–office styling and beauty service

Another mobile beauty option is to take your service to the office. You could offer treatments for clients during lunch breaks or they could have you arrive before hours to get them ready for the day, or they might book you to touch them up before an important meeting or interview.

It would be set up much the same as any mobile business except your focus would be hair, make-up and possibly nails. You would need to fit your equipment in one bag or a toolkit for ease of travel, as you are likely to be going up many floors and can't just rush back to your car to get more products.

You could promote this service as an addition to your current beauty business or have it as the sole purpose of your business. To gain business, contact companies and ask to be included in their newsletter as well as distribute flyers — once you get a few good clients, news of your service will spread by word of mouth. You can offer discounts if more than one staff member use your services at the same time.

You could charge $50 for a basic touch up or from $100 for a complete hair and make-up package.

332 Apply airbrush tattoos

Applying airbrush tattoos is easy to learn and set up. You need the machine, some stencils and ink. It will be easy to find models to practise on and once you have the hang of it you can do it at fairs, markets or in salons.

You will need a portfolio of your work so that people can choose a design they like, and you need to provide a comfortable chair and table for people to use when they are having their work done, and towels laid down to protect the area.

Setting up at markets and fairs would be the easiest way to get started, as well as leaving your business card with salons and offering to cross-promote. You can charge from $5 for a small design and upwards of $20 for larger ones.

333 Apply henna tattoos

Henna tattoos (*mehndi*) are a natural way to dye the skin. The henna dye comes from the henna plant and is very popular among Indian and Middle Eastern cultures. The patterns used have different meanings in different cultures but are often just used for fun in Western culture.

To learn how to do it you can ask someone with experience to teach you or teach yourself. There is quite a bit to learn to make the application last and to do it well.

Once you learn the skill and have sourced good-quality henna you can do it at markets, fairs or special events.

Henna is naturally red or brown but you mustn't be tempted to add black dye to the henna as this is extremely toxic and dangerous when applied to people's skin.

You can charge per hour or per design once you know how long each design will take you. The average hourly rate is about $70.

334 Provide a threading service

Threading is a technique that uses twisted cotton to rip hairs out instead of using wax. It is gentler on the skin than hot wax and very popular in Arabic countries, as well as in some other Eastern cultures. You can create very accurate lines and can pull out even very short hairs. It can be quite painful to start with but the more it is done the more your body can cope with the sensation.

There is a real art to doing it correctly, especially for eyebrows. You need to find someone experienced who can teach you and you will need a bit of practice.

Once you know how to do it you can work on a commission basis for beauty salons or start your own business. Areas with higher Arabic and Indian populations have an increased demand for it, so target those areas. You could also arrange to teach the skill with a class, or teach groups of hairdressers or beauticians in a beauty salon how to do it so they can offer the service.

You can charge from $10 for eyebrows or upper lips to $60 or more for the entire face.

335 Wholesale hair and beauty

While there are many wholesale hair and beauty outlets, many do not sell to the public and if they do, they don't offer a very big discount. Since most of the products are made overseas in countries such as China and can be sourced much more cheaply there than buying through the companies here, you could deal with the international suppliers yourself and sell products online or set up a warehouse to sell to the public.

A proper warehouse will be cheaper to rent than a shop in a mall, but you will need to promote your business heavily because customers won't be walking past all the time. You can do this by getting good signage so your business is as visible as possible and by making sure it features highly in search engine directories so you are easy to find online.

You can make $2 to $10 from each product depending on how cheaply you can import them and how much you can sell them for.

336 Work as a nail technician

To work as a qualified nail technician you do need to complete an accredited course, but it won't take long and this is work you can do from home. You can offer full acrylic or gel nails, simple manicures and pedicures, or party tips for formals and special occasions.

Since there are so many cheap nail bars around, it might seem like a competitive industry to break into, but if you are a good technician, your clients' nails will last longer and be of better quality and ultimately save your clients money.

To ensure quality work, use good products, such as Creative Nails, and get trained to use them properly.

You can advertise your work through magazines, online and at bridal expos. You can charge from $50 for good-quality nails.

337 Teach everyday make-up application

Not everyone knows how to apply make-up properly. You could run classes teaching the basics of make-up application, such as how to match and blend foundation and apply concealer and other make-up, as well as how to pick colours that will suit their complexion and which make-up is appropriate to wear during the day. You could also teach how to go from day make-up to night make-up easily.

You could run your classes through a community college, from a beauty salon or as a private consultation in a client's home.

At a community college you could charge from $100 for a two- to three-week course, for a lesson in a salon from $50 and for a private consultation from $60.

338 Teach make-up application to teens

The teen years can be such an awkward time, with many girls wanting to experiment with make-up but just not knowing how to go about it. Many mothers may not have the time to teach their daughters or are just unsure about what is appropriate for their age.

You could offer make-up parties where you teach the girls the basics of make-up application as well as good skin care, while also offering to teach alternative styles such as emo make-up if they are interested.

You could do it on a party basis within their home, as a one-on-one consultation or as part of your make-up business. You could charge $25 per person at a party, or charge from $40 for a one-on-one consultation.

339 Teach seniors how to apply make-up

Senior citizens are often unaware that they need to update their look. The make-up they have been wearing for the last 30 years may no longer suit them or is the wrong colour for their skin. Many people don't realise how much our skin changes in colour and texture as we age and that there are many techniques we can use to make ourselves look younger or more vibrant.

You could run classes or offer one-on-one consultations. To advertise your services you could go to nursing homes, retirement villages or places where elderly citizens visit, such as bingo or lawn bowls. You could run classes in groups for $25 per person or private consultations for between $40 and $60.

340 Host mother—daughter beauty days

A mother—daughter beauty day can be a great way to bring families together and spend some quality time with each other. You could provide your service within their home or offer it as a package in a beauty salon.

You could offer different packages from manicures and pedicures to full-day deals with facials, body wraps and massages. You could teach them beauty treatments that they could do for each other so they can continue pampering themselves together.

Contact counselling services and ask if they will promote you as a fun experience for mothers and daughters. Also distribute flyers and ask to be advertised in school newsletters. You could offer a donation to the school for every booking made through them, so it could also work out as a worthwhile fundraiser. You could charge from $100 for two hours of pampering.

341 Teach updo hairstyling

You needn't be a qualified hairdresser to teach updo hairstyling but it would certainly add value to the class. You can teach simple hairstyles such as pony tails and French braids right through to more elaborate updos.

You could run the classes through a community college or offer group classes at people's homes or from a studio. You will need to supply everything from bobby pins to hairdryers, or provide a list of necessary supplies and ask your students to bring them along to the class. Alternatively, you could create packs with everything in them for students to purchase.

If you teach through a community college, you could charge $80 for a half-day class to $150 for two to three evening classes of one to two hours, not including materials.

342 Become an image consultant

An image consultant works with people to essentially give them a makeover from head to toe. Clothing, make-up, hair and nails all get dealt with, and there are usually some confidence-boosting exercises to help improve self-esteem.

You don't need any specific qualifications for this work but you do need an eye for detail and have good fashion sense. You will help people create a style they feel comfortable with, one that is flattering and that can easily be updated.

For their new image you would help people buy a few classic pieces of clothing, teach them about beauty maintenance, and arrange for new hair and make-up that are easy for them to maintain and look good.

You could advertise through job agencies, online and in magazines—your best bet might be parenting magazines and online forums for mothers, who often need a bit of help in the first few years of motherhood to help them feel gorgeous again. You could charge from $500 for this service, with the client paying for any purchases that are made, such as clothing or make-up.

343 Provide budget extreme makeovers

Everyone loves the idea of having a complete makeover but few can afford it. There are many things that don't necessarily cost a lot and can change a person's look.

You could visit clients in their homes, sort through their wardrobe and select the clothing that is most flattering and what could go together, teach them some make-up skills using the make-up they already have, or make a few suggestions of what to purchase, show them a few new hairstyles they can do themselves, as well as provide a few healthy meal ideas and exercises to help them get in shape.

It is amazing what a difference just reshaping eyebrows, a bit of make-up and a new hairstyle can do to freshen up a look. If your clients are unable to afford new clothes, you could show ways to update an outfit with accessories they already own.

To get started you could run a competition through a radio station, newspaper or shopping centre with a makeover as the winning prize. This would let people know about your business and lead to future work. You can charge from $150 for this service.

344 Become a personal stylist

It's not just celebrities who hire personal stylists; many people hire a stylist to help them present their best selves, especially if they are involved in a large event or going for an important job.

To work as a personal stylist you will need a good eye for detail and to be completely up with fashion trends. A degree in fashion helps but isn't essential as this work relies more on your personal flair as a stylist.

To get started create a portfolio using friends and family that you can show prospective clients. You could offer your services free in some fashion boutiques to attract new clients. Also contact radio stations, magazines or newspapers to ask if you could run a competition through them with the winning prize being a free consultation with you, giving you great exposure with loads of free advertising. You could charge from $200 for two hours' work.

345 Teach bridal and formal photography

Bridal and formal photography can be hard work because you are usually dealing with stressed-out people. If you choose to teach others how to do this type of photography, you could also teach them the skills necessary to deal with highly emotional clients as well as all the photographic details.

Your students could come along to weddings to watch you work or you can just teach them in a class situation. Get students to think outside the square to create great photos instead of typical standing poses.

You could charge from $200 for a class at a community college or more if you are training them individually with you as a mentor (note that this doesn't apply if they are employed by you).

Part IX

MAKE MONEY
WITH WEDDINGS

Weddings can equal big money. Some of the ideas in this section require a bit of money to organise, but many can be done on a shoestring budget. Most items needed for wedding businesses can be sourced online very cheaply, making it easier to get started.

Wedding expos are an excellent way to gain exposure for any wedding business and these days there are many expos that you can attend. They will help get your name out there and enable brides to see what you do. Just make sure you have a good portfolio, as well as flyers and business cards ready to distribute. A great website to find expos in your area is <www.easyweddings.com.au/information/wedding_expos.asp>.

346 Import wedding dresses

You can buy wedding dresses cheaply in Asia and resell them here. You need to find a very reputable company to deal with—and accept their labour laws—but you can make a decent profit from each dress. Many designer dresses also have cheap knock-offs, which look the same without the designer price tag.

When you have collected a range of dresses you could sell them from your home, or garage if you set it up nicely, or you could resell the dresses online. You can either have a selection to choose from or offer a three-month delivery period, giving you time to order the dress and have it sent to you.

A great website that has many designers and options is Alibaba.com <www.alibaba.com>. Just type 'wedding dresses' in the search box and you will be directed to a whole range of options. You can then contact the supplier directly if you are interested. You can typically make from $500 from each dress.

347 Offer wedding dresses for voluptuous women

Many women with fuller figures find it hard to find wedding dresses that are reasonably priced and look good. Considering most designer dresses are a size 12 or below, which is not the size of the average Australian woman, without paying an arm and a leg you could import larger sized wedding dresses from China and resell them here and make yourself a tidy profit.

When looking for suitable options check the supplier's feedback and customer testimonials. A supplier who has sold tens of thousands of dresses is more likely to have a quality product compared with one with very little feedback and reviews. You could make upwards of $500 a dress.

348 Rent out your own wedding dress

Once you are married your dress tends to sit in your wardrobe for years, but you could rent it out. If it's a classic design, it could be popular for years. If you have a 1980s or other specific-era style dress, it could be rented out for fancy dress parties, or if you have a simple dress, it could be used for debutante balls. You need to be fine with other people wearing your dress and accept the possibility that your dress may be ruined or suffer from wear and tear.

Get a proper contract drawn up listing all the variables, including cost of hire, what happens if the dress gets ruined (for example, do you offer an insurance policy that they can choose to pay for to protect themselves against the full cost of replacing the dress), the length of time the dress can be rented, the cleaning of the dress, late fees and anything else relevant.

This option won't provide a constant form of money but it can make back what the dress cost you originally, possibly more. Depending on the style and popularity of your dress you can charge anything from $80.

3 4 9   Rent out wedding dresses and suits

Hiring is more cost-effective for people on a budget who want specifics like top hat and tails rather than buying their own clothing. If you import these items from Asia, your business can work out reasonably cheap to start up.

You will need to offer a variety of options so you have a full range to choose from. You could stock one of each style and then order the necessary sizes after the bridal party has been measured, which will make it easier and cheaper when you are getting started.

You will need to work out stipulations such as if the clothing needs to be returned dry-cleaned or if you do the cleaning, the length of time the clothing can be hired for, what happens if an item gets torn or damaged, do you provide an insurance excess that they can pay to cover any damages and so on. Consider all variables.

Creating a website with photographs of the styles you offer and sizing options would be greatly beneficial. After set-up costs you can make from $100 per suit or dress.

3 5 0   Rent marquees

If you have the space to store a few giant marquees and know how to set them up quickly and take them down, you could hire them out for weddings and parties. Since marquees are hired for everything from weddings and engagement parties right through to 21st birthdays and

Christmas parties, it can be a relatively simple way to make some money.

A white marquee is the most common variety as it is the most versatile and particularly suited to weddings. You could offer varying sizes of marquees that could be used for different-sized functions. As an extra service you could also hire heaters for the marquees.

Team up with other wedding services to cross-promote and get your name out there. Also consider doing a few functions for free when you begin to gain customer references and some photos for a portfolio.

Depending on the size of the marquee, whether you deliver and set up or if your clients pick up themselves, you can make from $200 for a 10- to 15-person marquee or up to $2000 for a large marquee suited to a wedding.

351 Decorate halls

Many couples hire halls because they are cheap venues for wedding receptions, but they are usually very plain. You could provide a service where you decorate the hall for them.

You could store everything you need from chair covers, tablecloths and sashes to theme items such as sea shells in labelled tubs in your garage. If flower arrangements are required, you could make connections with dealers at the flower markets to get them more cheaply.

You will need to decide which items can be kept by the bride, such as flowers, and which items must be returned to you.

For an extra fee you can offer to wrap and deliver any flowers and items the bride gets to keep after you have packed up the decorations when the wedding is finished.

To create a portfolio you could set up some tables decorated in a variety of different themes and take photos of your work. Also create a website to show the images and include all relevant information, such as contact details and prices, as well as a Facebook page. When you are organised contact community halls in your area to ask if they will recommend you to people who hire their hall.

Depending on the size of the wedding and decorations needed you could easily make $200 to $500, if not more, after all expenses have been paid.

352 Offer wedding reception entertainment

Today there are so many different wedding themes that you probably have a talent that could extend to entertaining at a reception. All sorts of talents are hired, from dancers and singers to different types of musicians, such as bagpipe players, pianists and harpists. For example, medieval weddings hire sword fighters, jugglers and roving minstrels.

Since weddings are usually an expression of the couple's personalities there is something for everyone out there. What you do and how long you will be there, as well as how unique your skill is, will determine the rate you can charge—on average you would earn $250 to $600 for a four- to five-hour wedding reception.

353 Become a wedding MC

If you are comfortable talking into a microphone in public and are quick-witted, you would make a great MC. You need to be friendly and sociable and it helps if you are charismatic.

As an MC you help ensure that the reception runs smoothly by announcing what is happening and where people need to be. You don't need any qualifications, just a good reputation and a black-tie suit. You need to be well presented, so proper grooming—hair, nails, make-up (if you are a woman)—is a must.

For recommendations you could contact wedding venues and possibly be included with their packages. You can make from $500 for a typical five-hour reception.

354 Play instruments at the wedding venue

If you play a unique instrument, such as a harp, you could perform while the bride walks down the aisle at her ceremony. Alternatively, some couples like to celebrate their heritage at their wedding and can do this through music, such as bag-pipes if they are Scottish.

All you need is the instrument you already play and a repertoire of songs you can perform for the occasion. You may only be required for half an hour or so to perform before and after the ceremony, but some wedding parties like to continue the theme and have you play when they enter the reception as well.

Depending on whether you are hired for half an hour or for a full ceremony you can earn from $100 to over $500 per wedding.

355 Work as an organist at weddings

If you are the church organist or pianist, you could arrange with the person who coordinates the hire of the church to be hired out as well to play the music for the occasion. This makes it easier to get 'in' and since you already have a reputation and play regularly at the church, people who may be interested in your service can see how you play and if they like your style.

This work would be done as more of a hobby occupation than a full-time job since you would also be playing during regular church services. You could easily make $100 to $200 depending on the length of the ceremony and the amount of playing required.

356 Become a wedding services guide

Creating a wedding guide for your local area may take a bit of time and effort to set up but would be well worth the effort. It could be done online as a website or blog, or published as a newspaper or magazine. It could be a collaboration of everything wedding-related in your local area or everything 'needed' for a great wedding.

Once you have decided how you will do it, you will need to contact all the wedding-related businesses that might be interested in an advertising package with you, which might contain one or all of the following:

☞ an article on the business to appear on the website or in the publication

☞ a colour photograph or two to appear with the article

☞ a discount offered for advertisements

☞ a banner to appear on the top, bottom or side of the website

☞ a discount for continuing the banner advertisement for the following month or year depending on how long you decide to run the website or publication for.

Work out your packages and present them in an attractive portfolio outlining what each package entails and how much it costs. When you are starting out you could generate a few hundred dollars that with time could roll into more than $1000 a month.

357 Work as a mobile make–up artist for bridal parties

A make-up artist who comes to the bride's home appeals to many brides who already have enough to do on their big day than spend precious time in a salon. For an extra fee you can offer to be present for the entire day to provide touch ups and prep for photo taking to ensure that the bride looks perfect all day.

Work out exactly which services you will provide and organise a contract. On the contract state your entire fee and details such as who you will be applying make-up for (for example, the bride, bridal party and bride's mother), which services will be covered, the colours/look chosen for the day, the amount of the non-refundable deposit that is to be made and when the final payment is due.

Arrange a trial and charge for it. This fee can be deducted from the total contract amount, but do not do it for free or you will be taken advantage of.

Initially you will have to spend to get a good supply of make-up as well as equipment such as brushes, sponges, an eyelash curler and tweezers, but you will recoup that expense quickly.

For a single bride you can charge from $60 for a trial and $100 for the actual wedding day make-up, and for bridesmaids $40 to $50 each or $200 for a maximum of five. To be present for the entire day you can charge $600 to $1000.

358 Work as a mobile bridal party hair stylist

This job is similar to working as a mobile make-up artist but instead you would be styling hair. This work will be easier if you are a qualified hairdresser, although there are hairstyling courses available for those specifically wanting to create updos for weddings and formals.

You will need a good portfolio of the styles you can create as well as a solid understanding of how to do different styles. The main tools you will need will be a hair straightener, which can also be used for curls, a curling wand, hot rollers, a hairdryer, hairspray, bobby pins, styling products such as shine spray, gel and wax, and a variety of brushes and combs.

A trial before the wedding day to determine the style the bride would like and how much work is involved should be arranged and charged for, usually at 50 per cent of the actually wedding day style cost. At this trial you should bring a contract to be signed that outlines the hairstyle that you have agreed upon, your fee, whose hair you will be doing and so on. You should be paid a non-refundable deposit at this point.

You can charge from $100 for a simple bridal style right through to upwards of $1000 to be present for the entire day.

3 5 9 Design wedding rings

Designing people's wedding rings to their specifications can be very time-consuming and stressful but you can charge accordingly. You will need to have some good contacts in the jewellery industry. You will also need to have completed a design course so you can draw the rings that the couple would like.

When completing the design you will need to prepare a contract outlining the actual design and stipulating payment for the various stages of the rings' completion, such as the deposit amount for the rings and then the final payment. The couple need to agree to the specific design you have drawn and the requirements of the contract.

To get started you could contact established jewellers and ask if they would be willing to refer you as a designer. Many jewellery chains do not design themselves but are frequently asked for this service. If they have someone to refer customers to this will improve their customer service and customer satisfaction.

For the amount of time involved it may not always feel worth it, but you could easily make from $1000 a ring.

360 Write wedding speeches

Not everyone can write a great speech. In fact, most people shudder at the thought of it. You could offer a set range of speeches in a book or on a website that they can choose from, or you could offer to create a personalised speech based around some anecdotes that your client supplies. This approach makes it look like your client wrote the speech themselves rather than grabbing it from a book.

You need to have a flair for words for this work. If you are good at giving speeches, it will be even easier for you.

It is a good idea to get a paid deposit for the speech upon consultation. At this time outline in a contract how long the speech is expected to be, details about what the speech is for, the stories that will be included and your deadline. Expect to charge around $50 a speech.

361 Create wedding vows

As with wedding speeches, not many people are good at writing wedding vows. There are many generic options available online, but you could offer a more personalised wedding vow service.

After some consultation with the happy couple you can make an agreement about how long the vows will be, when they will be ready, the amount of deposit required and when full payment is due. If they are happy with your services, ask if they are willing to write a referral or a customer testimony for you to use. You could charge around $50 for a set of vows.

362 Sell bridal party attire

It's not just the bride who needs clothing for the big day. Bridesmaids, the groom, groomsmen, page boys, flower girls, mother of the bride and more all need bridal party attire.

You could make the suits and dresses or import them. You needn't focus on just suits and dresses either. You could also sell accessories such as bags and hair pieces for girls or ties and cummerbunds for guys. Another option is to specialise in attire for various religious ceremonies.

It could cost a bit to set up, but if the quality of your clothing is good and reasonably priced, or has a point of difference, this could be very profitable. Depending on what you are selling and how much you are selling, you could reasonably make $100 or more from various outfits and less on accessories.

363 Arrange bridal flowers

If you have a flair for decorating with flowers, you could always consider bridal floristry. Since the price of flower arrangements jumps drastically when a wedding is mentioned, you could make a few hundred dollars per wedding.

In most areas actual floristry qualifications are not necessary. You can get your flowers directly from the markets and consult books and magazines to get ideas for arrangements.

When consulting with a bride it will help to have a portfolio with photos of the flowers that you use and images of your work. You will need to know which flowers are in season because out-of-season flowers cost a lot more. You will need to write a contract agreeing on what is being ordered, your total fee, the deposit to be paid and the design in which the flowers will be arranged. The deposit usually covers the cost of the flowers, so you won't be out of pocket.

It can be stressful dealing with brides. To make their day easier you could also offer a delivery service. You can charge $50 to $150 for a bouquet, usually making at least half that amount in profit.

3 6 4 *Preserve wedding bouquets*

More and more brides are choosing to keep mementos from their special day and preserving their bouquet is becoming increasingly popular. If preserving flowers sounds like something you would like to try your hand at, be aware that it is not a cheap exercise; however, it does produce a lovely piece of artwork—and can make you a decent profit.

You will need the proper equipment to freeze-dry the flowers and this can be a large initial outlay. You will also need to buy frames, be able to make frames or have a deal with a local frame maker. You can also include wedding photos or the marriage certificate in the frame for something different.

Depending on the size of the bouquet, the type of flowers and type of frame being used, the price will vary greatly. You can charge about $600 for small bouquets and more than $1000 for larger bouquets.

365 Put together wedding gift baskets

Gift baskets are easy presents for weddings, engagement parties, hens' and bucks' nights, and kitchen teas. You can simply adjust them according to the occasion. For example, honeymoon-themed hampers can include goodies such as massage oils, shower gel and bubble bath; house-themed hampers can be made up of items such as linen, kitchen utensils and gourmet food; and wine-themed hampers can contain champagne flutes engraved with the happy couple's names, a bottle of champagne and chocolates.

You could sell the gift baskets online and have them delivered or you could give customers the option of picking them up from your home. You could also offer extra services such as having the basket delivered to the couple's hotel suite before they arrive from the reception.

You can create a variety of hampers from those for the budget conscious through to all-out luxury. One option is to pre-fill the baskets or you could allow customers to select what they would like to include in the basket. Wrap the baskets in cellophane, tie a ribbon around them and attach a card.

Depending on the number of items in the gift basket and how much you have to outlay, you may only make a profit of $10 to $20 on small baskets or $50 on large baskets.

Marketing for free (and cheaply)

Now that you are ready to start your business you will need to promote it. When considering how to advertise a business, most people immediately think it is going to cost big money, but there are actually quite a few ways to advertise that cost nothing or very little.

↪ *Yellow Pages online.* This option is free, whereas if you wish to place an ad in the book it is quite expensive. There are other free classifieds websites online where you can list your business; Yellow Pages is just the biggest.

✑ *Place signs on community noticeboards.* You can make up a flyer yourself and stick it on a noticeboard. It is quite surprising how many community noticeboards there are. Check with whoever owns it that it is okay to advertise your business first, as not all allow it.

✑ *Do a letterbox drop.* Create a flyer and deliver it. It can take a long time to do and can be very hit and miss. Last time I did one about 10 per cent of the houses I delivered to became regular clients. You can deliver your flyers yourself or pay someone to do it for you.

✑ *Start a blog.* A website is better but even having a blog, which is free to set up, is very helpful for you to be found online. The first place people look for information about a business is online.

✑ *School newsletters.* If you have kids at school, ask if you can put an ad in their school newsletter. Some schools allow it, others don't. You could offer a product or service from your new business for the school to use as fundraising in exchange for the ad.

✑ *Cross-promoting.* This is incredibly easy, yet I am so surprised by the number of businesses that don't do it. Cross-promotion is when products are advertised together to increase the chances of a sale. You can do this two ways—firstly with your own products, making packages or recommendations of similar products or products that complement each other. The other option is to work with other businesses to promote each other's services. For example, when I worked in a beauty salon we cross-promoted with the local florist. We had an arrangement of their flowers on our front counter, which was changed regularly, and we displayed their business cards close by. We recommended them to all of our clients and in turn the florist recommended us, especially when they worked with bridal parties. It didn't cost either of us anything, as flowers used were fake and were changed weekly, but we both received customers we otherwise would not have got. In another beauty salon, the local chemist asked us to include a small advertisement for our business in their newsletter, which was distributed directly to over 1000 homes, in exchange for us recommending them as a chemist. And I used the chemist, so I wasn't lying to my clients when recommending them. Who could you team up with to cross-promote your business? Depending on the focus of your business, think about which businesses would complement it best.

▷ *Social media.* If you aren't a member of Facebook, Twitter, MySpace or Bebo, you should be — at the very least Facebook and Twitter. Many people use them, businesses have fan pages and this is how you will crack the younger demographic. They are free to set up and make it look like you are in the 'know', even if you aren't. There are also a variety of business directory fan pages on Facebook that you can join for free to get exposure.

▷ *Newspapers.* I'm not talking the classifieds; I'm talking special features. Often local newspapers will run features on subjects such as beauty, weddings, health and senior living. And they run 'articles' on various businesses that fit with these categories. They are usually cheaper than an advertisement and more likely to be read.

℈ *Signage on your car.* This varies greatly in price, but even a simple one with your business name and phone number is fine, and usually cheap. You drive anyway, so you may as well advertise yourself while you do it.

℈ *Run promotions.* These can be as simple as a promotion such as 'refer people to our business and for every third person who joins or uses our services you get $20 off the price'.

℈ *Loyalty cards.* This concept is really simple but very effective. You can offer something for free or half price for every tenth time a purchase is made or the service is used, depending on what you do. The deal can actually be printed on the back of your business cards so clients only need to carry one card.

℈ *Community assistance.* This doesn't have to be sponsorship—you can offer your time or help in some way and it is still a good promotion for your business. Giving time or services is just as appreciated as money and you will be seen within the community as a generous, helpful person.

℈ *Radio advertising.* This can get very expensive, depending on when and which radio station you are advertising with, but there are cheap packages out there. Local or community radio is usually the cheapest, but they don't necessarily have a large audience.

℈ *Shop window ads.* Approach various businesses and ask if they will display a flyer in their window advertising your business.

℈ *Signage in front of your house.* Even if your business isn't based at your home, everyone driving past will see your sign. And since you own your property, it's completely legal. Ask if family or friends who live nearby will do it for you, too.

⊅ *Email.* You should email everyone you know about what it is you do. Don't just email the people who live near you either because it might just be that someone you know who lives five hours' away has a friend or relative who lives in your area and needs your services.

⊅ *Bus stop and bus signage.* An ad on a bus stop can be quite effective if it's located on a busy road. People who drive past it regularly may not notice it consciously but it will often be subconsciously remembered.

⊅ *Wear a uniform.* When people see you working in your uniform they will see both your business name and the quality of your work. A uniform is free advertising and you have to wear clothes anyway.

⊅ *Get reviews.* You can offer free trials or products to reviewers, such as bloggers, in exchange for them writing a review about you on their blog. This has proven to be a very effective technique and is relatively cheap to organise.

⊅ *Media presence.* Offer to be on a radio show or featured in magazine so people can ask questions about what it is you do. This is sort of like a helpline, but based around your knowledge. Depending on your business this could be an excellent way to gain exposure.

There are many more ways you can advertise for free or very cheaply. Sit down and brainstorm ideas and you will be surprised what you come up with.

Solutions to excuses

There are so many reasons why people think they can't make money, many of which have simple solutions. Some of the excuses I hear all the time, such as 'I have children to look after', 'I have no time', 'I have no qualifications', 'I can't get motivated' and 'I'm not confident enough', I am going to help you solve right now.

I have children to look after

Child care can be a problem for many. It's expensive and hard to get your children into. Often it can end up costing as much as you are earning, which makes it seem pointless. I have two young children, so I am well aware of this issue. Here are some ways that you can get child care that don't cost you money.

⊃ *Do a baby-sitting co-op.* Get a group of friends and take turns looking after each other's children.

⊃ *Kid exchange.* If you and a friend want to work part time and you both have kids, if possible try to work alternating hours, so when you have time off you can care for each other's children.

⊃ *Swap the weekdays for the weekend.* Say you can only work at the market on weekends and a friend works weekdays, see if it's possible to pick up your friend's children from school daily and look after them instead of using after-school care in exchange for your children being cared for on the weekend.

⊃ *Barter.* Can you clean someone's house or mow their lawn in exchange for your children being looked after for a few hours when needed?

⊃ *Offer a school holiday program.* If you are at home during the holidays, you could offer to look after some friends' children. Having extra kids each day can be tiring, but you will quickly accumulate free child-minding hours if doing it in exchange.

⊃ *Offer to clean.* Could you offer cleaning services at a local childcare centre in exchange for some free childcare?

It might seem daunting at first to suggest any of these ideas to friends or people you know, but unless you ask, you'll never know if it could work for you.

I have no time

All of us are given the same amount of time every day; it is simply a matter of how we spend our time that results in what we achieve. Following are some things you can do to help set aside time to work on your money-making ventures:

> *Prioritise.* Work out what deserves your time most then plan things accordingly. My daughters deserve my time the most, so I have planned my routine around them. If you need to make money then plan your activities around that.

> *Develop a routine.* Mine is a very loose routine, more of a rough guideline, since things can change at any time. Basically the morning is spent going out to the park or whatever. We come home for my daughters to nap, during which time I work. The afternoon is variable, sometimes we go out, sometimes we sing and read books, then we make dinner and the girls go to bed. Once they are in bed I work again. I have been getting much more done knowing I have a short time frame in which to do things and I have been enjoying my daughters more since my work is confined to timeslots away from them.

> *Combine tasks.* When you do something, see if it can serve two purposes. For example, my daughters love to dance, so I dance with them. My eldest tells me how to do it and she is very active. I now consider this my workout time, because it uses every part of my body and gets my heart pumping. So instead of going for a one-hour power walk alone or going to the gym, I am spending time with my daughters and still exercising and saving myself one hour.

> *Get rid of the TV.* There are so many reasons to do this. It is one of the biggest time wasters. If you switch the TV off for a month, you will probably find that you miss nothing at all and end up with heaps of time on your hands.

➼ *Ask yourself if it is worth your time.* Many things we do are not really what we want to be doing and serve no real purpose. If it is not worth your time, stop doing it.

➼ *Remove guilt.* I have decided not to feel guilty about saying no to things I don't want to do. If I don't want to go to a café, I won't. If I don't want to travel three hours to go to a party, I won't. I do what I can, when I can, but I am not going to put myself into a spin trying to do everything for everyone.

➼ *Don't procrastinate.* Procrastination makes things build up and take longer than they should have. Take cleaning your bathroom, for example. If you do it regularly it is a chore, but shouldn't take too long. If you leave it for a few weeks, the mould, soap scum, toothpaste splatters and general gunk build, making the job take five times longer than it needs to. If there is something that needs to be done, just do it!

I have no qualifications

Lacking qualifications can make some work harder but it's not impossible to make money without them. There are many ideas in this book that can be done by anyone. You will be surprised at the things you can do that you can teach yourself, or find a mentor instead to guide you rather than do a full-time course.

If what you want to do does require study and a certificate, there are a number of ways in which you can achieve the qualification needed. These include:

➼ *Part-time schooling.* If you can only manage to study part time, you can choose from day or evening courses, and often TAFE full-time courses can be slightly flexible if you are able to do a lot of the schoolwork at home. A friend was able to achieve her diploma by attending classes part time even though she was enrolled in a full-time course. Her school understood the difficulties of combining study with work and children, so provided she completed all the work when it was due her teachers were happy to allow her the flexibility she needed. Ask your school about flexible learning options.

☞ *Distance education.* There are many courses you can study from home that allow you to submit your work online. It means you can work at your own pace, in your own time. They are often more expensive than other courses, but that is due to their flexibility.

If you can't afford the school fees, you can discuss payment options with the school, apply for scholarships, or check if you are entitled to any government assistance for education.

I can't get motivated

It can be hard getting and staying motivated but there are a variety of things you can do to help yourself. Here are some ideas:

☞ *Read a motivational book.* Depending on what I need motivation on determines which book I will read, whether it's finances, health or goal setting. My library is full of motivational books.

☞ *Exercise.* Going for a run, doing a gym class, swimming at the pool, anything that gets the blood and endorphins pumping will make you feel good, energised and refocused.

➪ *Look at your goals.* Check them regularly to see how far you have come and what you need to do now and reset your plans to help you achieve your goals.

➪ *Create a vision board.* A vision board is a collection of images and words of what you want to achieve. Having the images makes it more real and easier to visualise yourself achieving your goals.

➪ *Talk to someone.* If you have someone who knows about your goals, talk to them when you feel like giving up and they can help you see how much you've achieved or why you will achieve them and shouldn't give up.

➪ *Read blogs and websites.* Check all the online resources relevant to whatever it is you want to do.

➪ *Help someone else.* When I'm feeling down or lack motivation I find doing something for someone else takes the focus off me, clears my head a little bit, makes me value and appreciate what I have, and I feel better.

➪ *Listen to motivational CDs.* They are there to help motivate and inspire you. You can borrow them for free from your local library.

I'm not confident enough

Gaining confidence is not easy for everyone, yet some people seem to have so much of it they could share it with 20 other people and still have leftovers.

Not all super-wealthy people are successful every time they do something but that doesn't stop them. They don't let one, two or even 10 failures slow them down. They keep going because they have confidence in themselves. Take Sir Richard

Branson, for example. He started with Virgin Records and believed in himself. Has he been successful every time he's done something? No! *But* he does continue to try new things and look how successful he is.

You're not a confident person? Neither was I. I try to be and many people think I am and I know I'm more confident than some, but it hasn't been easy to develop self-confidence. In fact, it is an ongoing thing for me. Here's a list of things that have helped me gain more confidence that you can follow yourself:

- *Write a list of things you like about yourself or you are good at.* You can start with 10 things. I made myself write a list of 100, which wasn't easy at the time.

- *Re-read the list.* When you've written that list make a few copies and read them often. I put one copy in my wallet and taped one to my bedroom wall, one to my computer and one to my bathroom mirror. I used to read it whenever I felt any self-doubt or got stuck in negative self-talk.

- *Have a daily positive affirmation.* Say it out loud every day but a few times a day is best. Look in the mirror and say something such as 'I am a confident/sexy/ successful woman/man'. Say it strongly, with purpose and *mean* it.

- *Write a list of your achievements.* Recently when I was looking for ideas for my bucket list I was reading through other people's lists and was amazed by how many of the things that I had already achieved on their lists. I didn't think I had done much, but when I started writing down some of those things I was amazed and quite proud of my achievements.

➪ *Get positive feedback.* Ask people what they like about you and what they consider your good points to be. It might feel embarrassing at first, but if you are doing it with someone you trust and they know why you want to know, it's easier.

➪ *Learn to accept compliments.* When someone gives you a compliment just say thank you. Don't talk it down. If someone says they like your outfit, don't say 'This old thing? Oh, it's nothing', just say 'Thank you. I love it, too'. You can return the compliment, but stop putting yourself, your things, or your work down.

➪ *Record compliments.* When you receive a compliment, write down who you received it from and when. This is a definite record of good things about you. It will give you a boost when you need it too.

➪ *Stop the negative self-talk.* We are our own worst critics. Whenever you start to think negatively about yourself, whip out your list of things you like about yourself or your list of compliments and read it. If you are not in a position to do that, just change what you are thinking. It can be hard at first, but try to remember your achievements and the good things you like about yourself. Think of your daily positive affirmation and repeat it over in your head.

➪ *Take care of yourself.* Many people are guilty of neglecting themselves, especially when you are a parent. We get so caught up in everything else, we forget about ourselves. Often when we are young we spend a lot of time doing our hair and make-up, dressing well, wearing perfume and exercising regularly. Then life happens and we get too busy, or we just do the basics. Give yourself a break and start taking care of yourself again. The confidence you'll gain from just a good hairstyle and a well-put-together outfit will feel fantastic.

⚏ *Think positive thoughts.* While for many this is easier said than done, it is so important. Changing the way you think about everything, not just yourself, will have an astounding effect on your own life and the world around you.

⚏ *Act positive.* Being happy, smiling and giving compliments will make you feel better about yourself and make thinking positively a whole lot easier.

⚏ *Be prepared.* Study and know your stuff. When you know what you are talking about and what you have to do, you will approach everything with much more confidence than if you are unprepared.

⚏ *Be true to yourself.* What are your standards, principles or values? What do you live by? Without principles we have no guidelines or direction for our life. Having no direction gives you no reason for confidence since you aren't working towards anything. When you have direction and aim, you are more confident because you know what you are doing.

⚏ *Do what you love.* Whatever it is, do it regularly. Doing something you love, such as cooking, swimming, gardening, piano or painting, gives you positive feelings about yourself that can then overflow into other areas of your life. The happier you are and the more you achieve, the more confidence you will have.

⚏ *Meditate.* This might sound stupid to a lot of people, but just spending some time sitting still, quietening your thoughts and slowly breathing in and out can really help you.

▷ *Set some goals and achieve them.* To begin with your goals might be as simple as paying your bills on time or writing a to-do list that includes grocery shopping, banking and returning library books that you must complete by the end of the week. Having goals gives you something to strive for. Starting with small goals gives you mini confidence boosts when you achieve them. Having big goals to work towards gives you direction. If you break those big goals into subgoals, every time you achieve one you will be a success.

▷ *Recognise what makes you feel insecure.* Why are you insecure about it? What can you do to change it? Me, I am insecure about dancing. It strikes fear into my heart, but the dancing I do daily with my girls helps me loosen up and feel unselfconscious since they think I am fabulous no matter what my crazy moves look like.

▷ *Keep good posture.* Standing up straight and ensuring your back is straight makes you look confident — it is confident body language. When you are projecting confidence you can't help but feel confident.

▷ *Get rid of toxic friends.* What are toxic friends? They are the ones who are always negative, leaving you to question yourself and what you are doing. They don't encourage you, they just tear you down. They are often people who have been in our lives for quite a while, so we don't realise how bad they are for us. Also, they are *not* really friends.

▷ *Focus.* When you are focused, you are studying, getting to know what you need to do and doing it. This leads to achievements and success, which leads to more confidence.

A final word

I hope you have enjoyed this book and have found it useful. There are endless possibilities to make money, sometimes we just have to think outside the square. There is no reason why you can't make money in some form or another from any of the ideas in this book.

While the amount you earn may not be much to start with, you can easily make it grow. There are so many good books and websites out there that will help you make money and learn more about finances. Making money is the first step. Managing your money is the next.

I had a lot of fun compiling this book. If you would like even more ideas and advice, check out my website at <www.kylieofiu.com>.

The 365 ways to make money